W9-BRS-591

Holidays and Other Disasters

John G. Rodwan, Jr.

Holidays and Other Disasters

HUMANIST PRESS

WASHINGTON, DC

Copyright © 2013 by John G. Rodwan, Jr.

Humanist Press
1777 T Street NW
Washington, DC, 20009
(202) 238-9088
www.humanistpress.com

Printed book ISBN:9780931779398
Ebook ISBN: 9780931779411
Editor: Luis Granados
Cover design: Lisa Zangerl

TABLE OF CONTENTS

INTRODUCTION

As if there were a massive party going on at multiple locations all at once and everyone was invited, festiveness enlivened the city. We'd wandered into something special. Smiling people filled cafés and restaurants; stores hosted what seemed like more than mere wine-tastings. It didn't take long to discern the reason for the celebration. Indeed, all it took was reading the signs:

Le Beaujolais nouveau est arrivé

My wife and I moved to Europe on our first wedding anniversary. A few weeks later, we took our first trip to Paris together. While there, we stopped in a shop in the Latin Quarter, sampled the fresh grape and bought a bottle to share back at our hotel. We also bought a collapsible corkscrew that we carried with us on subsequent trips around the continent. After we returned to the States, we continued to buy each year's Beaujolais nouveau. Sometimes we gave bottles to friends and shared our story of stumbling upon an urban harvest carnival in the lively heart of France.

Superficially, at least, our tradition has many trappings of actual holidays. It recurs annually. It has deep historical roots. It sees friends and family gathering. It involves shopping. More significantly, the third Thursday of every November is fertilely symbolic. Beaujolais nouveau uncorked that day serves as an emblem of new beginnings. We associated the harbinger of what to expect with the next vintage with the start of our life together in a new place. It wouldn't take much imagination to see behind this practice the identical impulse underlying routine religious observations. Treating the arrival of the fruit of agricultural labor as notable means recognizing the momentousness of seasonal progression, something a friend who received the wine from us and heard our reason for giving it regularly worried was something many people no longer did. It simultaneously heralds continuity (it happens every year) and change (it's different each time). Cyclical appreciation of the newness declared in the wine's very name hints at the solemnization of resurrection and renewal on days like Easter and Christmas. And pageants held on those days also treat wine as something more than only something to drink.

Yet as someone who chafes against many holidays and their rituals because of the inadequacy of religion to explain what it presumes to explain and because of the real foulness it often inflames in its followers, I always thought our modest fêtes differed in essential ways from those days. We embraced newness, not numinousness. Our acknowledgement of the beautiful possibilities of incipience represented viticulturally neither had nor needed supernatural supplements. We invited no gods to the celebrations we initiated a year after being married by a judge in my parents' living room. The wine resulted from human effort, not magic.

Still, I recognize that those who enact rituals can't always control how they're interpreted – or warped. Other commemorative occasions (like Labor Day) that required none had religious elements grafted onto them. Still others (like Thanksgiving) have a definite religious foundation that celebrants often elect to ignore, or disguise. Even civic quasi-holidays have seen unnecessary religious dressing draped over them. For example, when Francis Bellamy, in 1892, wrote "I pledge allegiance to my flag and the republic for which it stands, one nation indivisible, with liberty and justice for all," he did not include the words "under God." As David Greenburg explains in a *Slate* article, President Dwight Eisenhower signed a bill making the religion-promoting change on June 14, 1954 – Flag Day. To recite the modified version is to express, sincere ly or otherwise, commitment to enshrined religious as well as political ideals.

Our autumnal toasts stood apart from widely recognized holidays (and the sneaky sanctimony of the revised pledge) by entailing no compulsion. We freely adopted the yearly habit and expected nothing from anyone else. Traditions may not be inherently bad, but they aren't automatically good either, and a core part of me rebels against doing things simply because others have long done them. We never assumed anyone would share our Beaujolais noveau sentiments. If friends so chose, they could drink some wine with us and listen to an anecdote from early on in our couplehood, but no one needed to participate in events that held meaning for us but not for them. Upholders of major holidays' traditions usually don't extend the same courtesy – or even consider that not everyone shares their beliefs or, like non-believing go-alongs, the willingness to go along.

So, if my household's Beaujolais nouveau habit doesn't qualify as a holiday, why begin a book about holidays (and other disasters) with it? I do so for several reasons, not the least of which is what the differences between my personal routine and ceremonial conventions reveal. What I like about my not-quite-holiday – personal meaningfulness, deliberateness, secularity, voluntariness and perhaps even an air of cosmopolitanism – highlights what I dislike about many actually existing holidays – impersonal blandness, unthinking conformity, piety, required or expected participation, and stultifying parochialism.

Additionally, I want to demonstrate that a nonbeliever's unwillingness to celebrate religious holidays doesn't signal a rejection of what I'll call, for lack of a better term, the holiday spirit. I'll take the wine even as I deny that it is or represents holy blood. Conviviality and the perpetuation of traditions seriously considered and deemed worth perpetuating are good things. Indeed, I've known many people willing to go through the standard holiday routines because of the social-

- 3 -

izing amid seasonal decorations that goes along with them as if the spiritual side could be easily discarded. As these pages make plain, I'm not one of those people. As I believe they also show, I'm not a gloomy misanthrope either – not all the time anyway.

The main reason for opening with an example from personal experience is because this is a book of true stories about specific individuals. In most instances, the stories are my own, but when other people (like the writer Salman Rushdie and the boxer Jack Johnson) have especially revealing holiday stories, I tell those. Here I (usually) don't confront religious thinking with vigorously incisive, scrupulously logical arguments against it in the manner of polemicists like Christopher Hitchens (who does turn up a couple times). Instead, I describe what it's like to admire Martin Luther King, Jr., without sharing his theology, and to be an atheist in Catholic school. I explain what I don't like about parades and what I do like about Halloween. I recount my failed (and admittedly half-hearted) attempt to revive a forgotten regional holiday – one that, as it happens, formerly fell around Beaujolais nouveau time. I do this because I know reason won't shake convictions formed without it. ("To argue with a person who has renounced the use of reason is like administering medicine to the dead," as Thomas Paine put it.) I do it also because of my confidence – my faith, if I may – in the importance of individuals and in their ability to understand each other through stories.

These stories involve more than god-shadowed calendar squares, as some of the names cited in the above paragraph indicate. While religion inspired many holidays and infected several others, holidays expose more than a nation's religiosity. They are not only (or always) pageants of piety. Martin Luther King Day and the Fourth of July, for instance, both relate significantly to race in America. Thorough exploration of all the relevant elements and what they reveal about holidays' observers involves considering war, literature, music, sports and other expressive activities. Because events and rituals associated with certain other days not technically holidays help to illustrate the holiday mentality, I write here about a couple of them (in addition to the third Thursday in November). Nonetheless, uncritical wishful thinking and widespread assumption that everyone should partake of it unite these days, and this is what they look like to one skeptic.

KING AND ME

When I was young, my grandfather told me that for retired people like him, holidays are like any other days except more places are closed. I came to see school and business closures as the essential features of holidays. As someone who grew up with no belief in any god, I came to regard the traditional days of semi-obligatory celebration, most of which have a religious underpinning, with weariness and occasional annoyance. Unthinkingly following tradition – doing things simply because others have done them and have been doing them for a long time – never made much sense to me. However, I also found something appealing in the prospect of a new holiday offering more than free time with nothing to do. If a day were designated for a worthy secular reason, and there were no established rituals, routines and annual fifty-percent-off sales associated with it, then maybe some traditions that deserve to be respected could be started. Instead of simply doing what has always been done, people could be thoughtful about the newly designated day of celebration and it wouldn't be just another day off with ugly decorations. Perhaps a new holiday could be made meaningful, precisely because there would be no firmly entrenched tradition to follow. That was the hope, anyway.

One major day of observation has been set aside so far in my lifetime. The person whose life and legacy it enshrines certainly warrants recognition and his legacy deserves reflection, but the holiday itself probably has not realized its supporters' hopes for it. In 1983, President Ronald Reagan signed a bill establishing the third Monday of January as the day to observe Martin Luther King, Jr.'s birthday as a new holiday beginning in 1986, or about halfway through my junior year of high school.

When I was born, at the end of the year in which King was assassinated, U.S. soldiers were fighting in Vietnam. My mother and father, admirers of King, hoped I would never end up being drafted or voluntarily enlist in any branch of the military. I was never allowed to play with toy guns or tin soldiers. My parents hoped that I would be able to claim conscientious-objector status, should that ever become an issue. When I reached the age when military recruiters would call our house, my mother would tell them I wasn't home even if I were next to her when she picked up the telephone. As I approached my eighteenth birthday, I started getting cards in the mail reminding me to register with the Selective Service. I ignored the notices until a letter came with all the information the government required of military aged men already filled in, requesting that I simply verify its accuracy. I wondered why they did not do that in the first place rather than repeatedly telling me to go to the post office to provide personal data already on file. I actually received two sets of postcards, one with my name spelled correctly. After I returned the letter that showed that the government already knew where to find me, mail continued to arrive for a nonexistent teenager with a name very close to mine. Seeing these regular demonstrations of bureaucratic inefficiency, I never worried too much about being drawn into the military, were the draft ever reinstated. I had the opportunity to go to college and never contemplated joining the military on my own.

Now I can't say with certainty whether I support the idea of an all-volunteer military because there is something very honorable about a defensive force made up completely of men and women who choose to be a part of it or because it meant I never had to make the sort of difficult choices regarding military service that my parents' generation did.

Despite my parents' efforts and King's example, I never could have honestly claimed that religious beliefs would have made it impossible to serve in the military. Like Christopher Hitchens, I regard myself not only as an atheist who does not believe but also as an "antitheist" who maintains "that all religions are versions of the same untruth" and that "the influence of churches, and the effect of religious belief, is positively harmful," as he put it in 2001's *Letters to a Young Contrarian* (and repeated with slight variations in several subsequent books). I prefer to have evidence for what I believe and favor questioning and critical analysis over faith and irrational devotion.

The sensibleness of eschewing religion is so obvious to me that sometimes I wonder why it should require any explanation. Why should I have to recount the atrocities committed in the name of religions – throughout history and continuing today – when I am aware that doing so would not persuade those eager to brush off horrors committed by the faithful as perversions of "true" religion? Why should I have to enumerate the instances in which religions have fought against human development – by countering scientific investigation of the physical world and education based on related findings, for example – to point to the ways it has hurt rather than helped mankind? Why should I have to list the myriad contradictions that make literal belief in so-called Holy Scripture nonsensical (and why can't I resist doing exactly that)? Why should I have to justify my lack of belief or to rehash the already well-documented history of fiascoes related to belief in fairy tales?

I've always felt the burden of proof lies with the believers. I would need a reason to believe in God, any god, and to accept all that seems to come along with religion – the persecution and violence, the disregard of evidence, the veneration of faith over intellect – and I have not seen one yet. While King was a very persuasive rhetorician, nothing he ever said of a religious nature convinced me. Although I know many devoted activists of the civil rights movement were intensely committed to their religious belief, such belief was not required in order to work for justice. Furthermore, I am not a pacifist. Although King and others (including some nonbelievers) demonstrated the real power of nonviolent civil disobedience in certain situations, I still believe there are times when fighting is necessary. I believed that when I was eighteen and I never stopped believing it. But my thoughts about these issues were never put to the test. The United States was not at war when I was a teenager and there were sufficient volunteers for the peacetime military. What I thought about God and war didn't matter.

I cannot begrudge soldiers the holidays intended to honor them, and it seems appropriate that the one that's supposed to commemorate the war dead, Memorial Day, is given more weight (according to my grandfather's definition) than the broader Veterans Day later in the year, which acknowledges all who served in the U.S. military at any time. (Secular humanist Kurt Vonnegut claimed that Armistice Day, the predecessor of Veterans Day, was "sacred" in a way that its replacement is not. I take his complaint to be that Armistice Day celebrated the end of a war – World War I – and was not a general celebration of warriors like the holiday that now holds its former spot in November.) Still, I don't feel encouraged to think about honor, courage, patriotism, sacrifice and the other soldierly virtues when Memorial Day rolls around. I never was close to anyone on whose grave I should now put a flower or a flag; there are no particular individuals I knew for me to remember on this day in May. Any memorializing would involve abstractions rather than personal connections. Even in the first years of the twenty-first century, when U.S. soldiers were again engaged in combat, I still felt somewhat removed from all things military. I'd read about the fighting going on in Afghanistan and Iraq, but not one of my friends or relatives was there. The holiday probably means more to soldiers, veterans and their families than it does to someone like me, who respects the military and those who join it but who has no immediate, intimate involvement with members of the armed forces.

I do not feel this sort of distance from Martin Luther King

Day. For me, who grew up in predominantly black city (Detroit) where I was not part of the majority, there was nothing difficult to grasp about the new holiday. (Although King's "I Have a Dream" speech became identified with the August 1963 March on Washington, King delivered a version of it two months earlier in Detroit, and Motown founder Berry Gordy released a recording of it on an affiliated record label.) Detroiters recognized King as an effective advocate for justice and knew the country was better off because of his actions. It became clear to me that people elsewhere did not feel the same way. Dr. King was a heroic figure, and the idea that some would oppose a day for reflection on his aims and deeds seemed the epitome of the sort of racism he had hoped people would someday overcome. Twenty years after the first Martin Luther King National Holiday was celebrated in the seventeen states that recognized it, *The Atlantic Monthly* issued a list of the 100 most influential figures in American history. King ranked eighth, behind Chief Justice John Marshall and ahead of Thomas Edison. "His dream of racial equality is still elusive," the magazine noted, "but no one did more to make it real." To me, and my family, and the people I knew, it seemed obvious that both King's dream and his efforts to make it real warranted a holiday.

Yet what I remember most of its first years was controversy about the states that refused to recognize the holiday. There were protests calling for boycotts of places like Arizona. People were urged not to visit or spend money in such states.

A few years later, when I was in college, I remember walking to class on a day when I didn't think classes should have been held – the third Monday of January. I ran into someone I did not know at all but recognized as a classmate and commented that classes should not be in session. Having no idea what I was referring to, she asked why I felt that way. When I explained, she gave me a look of disgust that I can recall to this day. She quickened her pace to get away from me. This was on the campus of a small liberal arts college. The student body was mostly white, but it was not the sort of place where one would expect peers to have an obvious and strong aversion to the idea of a day off in honor of a black man who struggled for equality. I don't remember ever speaking with that young woman again. Perhaps she hailed from the last hold-out among the states, New Hampshire, where the motto imprinted on license plates reads "Live Free or Die." That state finally accepted the holiday in 1999.

A decade or so after that collegiate interchange, I found that resistance to King Day persisted, even in New York City. The first (and only) job I had there after a stint living overseas was at an office that closed for a certain number of holidays each calendar year. A memo listing each holiday would circulate in December. Generally, the expected days were indicated and there would be one holiday in just about every month (except August). However, if Christmas or Independence Day were to fall on a Tuesday or a Thursday, the practice was to add the day that preceded or followed the holiday in order to create a four-day weekend. This could have resulted in more days off in one year than another. Near the end of a year in which the office had closed for King Day, the holiday list arrived without the third Monday of the upcoming January on it. It was dropped in order to extend another holiday without increasing the total number of days off.

I protested at a staff meeting. Being told that I could take a personal day – the time allotted for things like doctor's appointments or other matters that necessitated time away from the office – did not satisfy me. I said the office should be closed in honor of Dr. King, and that it was doubly insulting to ignore the holiday after having closed for it previously. The short-term solution, or the attempt to mollify me anyway, for the new year was to give individual employees the option of taking either the holiday in January or one of the other not-regarded-as-essential ones (like Good Friday or Columbus Day) later in the year, but not both. Subsequently, King Day regularly appeared on the list.

Perhaps it seems strange for one who derides and dismisses religious conviction to admire a man with "Reverend" regularly situated in front of his name. There's no mystery. King's dedication to the ideals of America's promise as well as his commitment to peaceful means of trying to secure them may have sprung from or found support in his religious convictions. (A. Philip Randolph, by the way, had promoted and practiced nonviolent civil disobedience in efforts to integrate the armed services during the 1940s, when King was still a schoolchild, and he did so as a secularist.) Yet seeing the sheer stupidity of racism requires no faith in a god. As his involvement in the 1963 march and earlier ones organized by atheist and Humanist Manifesto-signer Randolph shows, King was willing to walk alongside anyone, regardless of his or her religious beliefs, who hoped to see the country move toward embodiment of the principles of freedom, justice and equality so eloquently given expression (if not realized) by Thomas Jefferson and the other founders, and we all ought to be able to do that much.

That former classmate of mine provides a model of what to avoid doing. There are some fundamentals without which a just society is impossible – we cannot treat some human beings as inferior to others because of skin color, for example – but we don't have to agree on everything. If we make perfect agreement a precondition for affection or regard, then we'll never care for anyone. Some zealous believers demand eschatological unanimity and choose violent methods of achieving it; that creates problems that my nonbelief does not. We can aim to make existence in this world more tolerable, more bearable, without holding the same views about how we got here. (Without abandoning his atheism, Randolph helped to coordinate and participated in the 1957 Prayer Pilgrimage. This Washington D.C. march in support of the civil rights bill then pending before Congress, held on the third anniversary of the Supreme Court's *Brown v. Board of Education* school desegregation decision, contributed to King's rise to national

UNBELIEVABLE GOD SONGS

God has smiled on me. I do not know what I've done to deserve even one of the kindnesses he has shown. I do know that Jesus is going to be here, and he is going to be here soon.

I do not believe any of the statements in the paragraph above – not a single one. I do, however, thoroughly enjoy the songs from which I have adapted them.

It may seem peculiar for a nonbeliever to find anything meaningful in religious music, but it really is not so hard to get hit in the soul by such songs. The emotions given voice in songs about God can be real, even if the ideas about the way the world works do not always hold up under scrutiny. Conventional gospel as well as jazz, blues and country style god songs can express those true and deep feelings with undeniable intensity and exuberance. Hope that circumstances will improve, that if you endure your current suffering you will enjoy better times later on – the central concept of many god songs – can speak to you even if you reject the celestial trappings. Sometimes, if you do not subscribe to the notion that an anthropomorphic almighty power intervenes in human affairs, you simply have to be able to take Jesus as a metaphor. Some songs – especially the ones about sinners who know they have done wrong and who need help to find the right path – make a more forceful impact if the forlorn figures seeking assistance are truly on their own in the wilderness from which they cry out. Many songs of an explicitly religious nature are ultimately about what it is to be human, to suffer and struggle, to be alone.

Amina Myers sings about a very beneficent and kind deity on trumpeter Lester Bowie's 1978 album *The 5ᵗʰ Power*, one of the first albums I remember buying that included a traditional religious song, albeit one arranged to fit extended free-jazz soloing. In "God Has Smiled on Me," the deity does not only signal his favor for the songstress with a friendly facial expression; the true sign of his love is his releasing her from bondage. "He has set me free," she proclaims. Set aside the dubious theological premises of the statement and its core message remains comprehensible: when things are going right, when you experience luck greater than you could have reasonably hoped for, when you have survived a grueling trial, saying God has smiled on you poetically captures the gist of the feeling.

For a time, Bowie was married to another singer, Fontella Bass, who brought gospel sounds and sentiments to jazz recordings made by him and by others, including the World Saxophone Quartet. After years of sticking to the four-horn ensemble structure their name denotes, the group eventually made some records along with other musicians playing percussion instruments, for example, or singing. Bass joined them for *Breath of Life*, and on the title track she recounts how God created all human beings as equals, precisely the kind of idea that made god songs such a prominent part of the civil rights movement. Just as one can oppose racism and advocate freedom without devotion to any imagined higher power, a listener can value anthems of emancipation while remaining firm in unbelief. If saying that when God put the breath of life into me it was the same thing he did to you, as Bass does, needs to be taken literally as an explanation of how human beings came into existence – forget what you may have heard about evolution! – then we might have a problem. However, it does not have to be interpreted that way. It can instead be heard as an artful expression of fellowship, or a plea for it.

Performing some of the songs most closely associated with the civil rights movement, Mavis Staples put together a record that made numerous music critics' lists of the best CDs of any genre in 2007. The Freedom Singers join her on *We'll Never Turn Back* for songs such as "On My Way," "This Little Light of Mine," and "99 and ½"; Ladysmith Black Mambazo contributes background vocals on tracks including "Eyes on the Prize." In the liner notes for the album, Staples is adamant about both the role of the church in the struggle against racial prejudice and the importance of organized religion in her singing. Staples says she and others in the movement "looked to the church for inner strength and to help make positive changes." I would have thought that individuals looked inward rather than upward for inner strength. However, she insists that many "drew on the spirituality and the strength of the church" in their quest for equal rights. I do not question, nor do I wish to question, the authenticity of her devotion, the sincerity of her statement, or even its historical accuracy. As a practical matter, after all, church buildings themselves provided places for activists to meet, share information and organize. Moreover, the involvement of ministers in protests and boycotts went some ways toward undermine opponents' attempts at red-baiting, as Jeanne Theoharis points out in *The Rebellious Life of Mrs. Rosa Parks* (2013), a biography of another civil rights movement stalwart who didn't give herself enough credit for the power of her own will, claiming instead that a deity was the source of it.

Then again, opponents of the civil rights movement, like opponents of Abolition before them, were no less inclined than its supporters to invoke religion to back up their positions, and White Citizens' Councils were heavily church-centered too.

Prior to the Civil War, proponents of enslaving Africans and their New World descendants routinely turned to scripture for support. They commonly turned to the book of Genesis (9:18-27) and the tale of the scattering of Noah's sons and their offspring to different areas of the Earth. When doing so, they associated Canaan, Noah's grandson through Ham, with Africa and blackness, and Noah's cursing him to perpetual slavery as Biblical endorsement of the institution. "In the context of American slavery," Fay Botham writes in *Almighty God Created the Races* (2009), "American Bible readers interpreted

- 17 -

this story of 'Noah's curse' and the dispersion of Noah's sons as a justification and explanation for racial slavery." The Bible, they believed, authorized slavery.

The end of legal slavery hardly ended pro-segregation arguments invoking God. "Indeed, a most pervasive theme in the history of white supremacy in America has been the readiness of its advocates to swaddle their beliefs in the holy writ," as Neil R. McMillen put it in *The Citizens' Council* (1994). "The scriptural defense of bondage was a mainstay of the antebellum proslavery argument. Nor did the theological defense of human subordination atrophy with the advent of abolition." If segregation was sanctioned by divine authority during biblical times, and many White Citizens' Council members had no doubt about that, then it remained so in the modern age. White segregationists openly, even ecstatically, professed their racist religious convictions. According to McMillen, "pro-segregation gatherings frequently exhibited all of the religiosity of old-fashioned revival meetings." He describes as typical one 1958 meeting in Montgomery, Alabama, where after the preacher declared separation of the races to be God's law, listeners were moved to respond, "Amen." A couple years earlier, of course, Rosa Parks and other determined opponents of separation of the races protested it with a lengthy boycott of the bus system in the very same city.

After the Civil War, the "dispersion" story, perhaps even more than the "curse" story, became justification for ongoing segregation and inequality. God created and separated different people, this interpretation went, as part of a plan; to end segregation, then, would be to defy God's will. Fay cites numerous examples of ardent Southern segregationists from the nineteenth century through the end of the twentieth who invoked this theology of race as the reason for continued separation of supposedly different groups with different natures. Ideas of racial divisions derived from Genesis were used to explain laws against interracial marriage, among other forms of segregation, such as the rules regarding where black and white riders could sit on Montgomery buses.

proved an undying source of inspiration for Cash. He joined the massive choir of country artists who recorded Kris Kristofferson's "Why Me." Cash called the iteration of it on his first *American Recordings* release "Why Me Lord." The certainty that you have done too much wrong to deserve affection or generosity from someone else, the desperation that accompanies the conclusion that you have wasted what another person has given you, and the shock that that someone remains willing to stand by you – all of that intense swirl of sentiment and suffering and joy is captured in Kristofferson's lyrics and in Cash's vulnerable delivery of them. The "Lord" that Cash added to the title need not exist for a listener to have that uncanny sense that the song articulates moments from his or her own emotional biography.

Kristofferson provides instances of a powerful song that can touch even the godless, but he also has penned at least one god song that could make even a true believer cringe. Kristofferson sang "Why Me" with George Jones in what to me was the high point of their joint Carnegie Hall concert in October of 2006. Earlier that same evening, he sang a protest song from the then-new album *This Old Road* that, however well intentioned it might be, relies on one of the most insidious aspects of religious belief: the unshakeable conviction that God supports my position and, thus, not yours. The poorly conceived "In the News" denounces such behavior, but also engages in it. Apparently referring to the war in Iraq, Kristofferson laments that "Everyone says God is on his side" – clearly an explosive problem. However, the singer also relates what he swears God said to him, which, of course, agrees with his own views on the war. God really is on *his* side, you see. Whether protesting war or racism, claiming you have a deity on your team is a nettlesome and possibly self-defeating act. As both American history and South African history show, anyone can say the same thing; it neither proves nor achieves anything positive.

In addition to revisiting canonical hymns and modern god songs like Kristofferson's (as well as secular pieces) during his fruitful period working with producer Rick Rubin on the numerous *American Recordings* albums, Cash also transformed what did not seem like devout material into his brand of sacred song. Depeche Mode's "Personal Jesus" always sounded to me as ironically intended rather than earnest. The 1980s pop group, I thought, mocked the idea of every person getting exactly the god he or she desired. Yet Cash felt he had a personal relationship with his lord. The feelings of helplessness and the need for aid and comfort that underpin his interpretation give it an emotional heft that the original lacks. He really did want someone to hear his prayers, someone who cared, and he really believed he had found such a figure. I may see life as a matter of persisting without recourse to cosmic kindness or a supernatural friend, but that does not keep me from being moved by Cash admitting his weakness and asking for help.

Indeed, for the faithless, god songs like Cash's can gain extra poignancy. When he says God reached down his hand or is calling, softly and tenderly, for you and me, he sincerely means it. Whether in the form of reworked secular pop songs or haunting, acoustic renderings of old hymns, Cash gives voice to a profound loneliness and the search for consolation from a heavenly father. That figure's absence makes Cash's isolation and longing especially resonant. His calling out for someone who is *not* there and is *not* going to lift him up or reunite him with those who have died makes his suffering more affecting than if what he so wanted to believe –what he did believe – were actually real.

While Cash may have pondered loneliness in many songs, he had company among fellow faithful artists who reimagined work by nonreligious artists. I have no idea whether Tom Waits truly believes Jesus once walked the earth and will return imminently, but when I first heard him so proclaim on the brutally brilliant *Bone Machine*, I heard the song as a three-minute distillation of *Waiting for Godot* rather than a straight statement of conviction. Played alongside tracks like

"Earth Died Screaming," "Dirt in the Ground," and "Murder in the Red Barn," his "Jesus Gonna Be Here" does not impart unqualified optimism about the future. When the Blind Boys of Alabama perform his song, however, you know they mean exactly what they say (though they leave out Waits's line about being good except for drinking). They include "Jesus Gonna Be Here" on an album, *Spirit of the Century*, mixing their takes on traditional fare like "Good Religion," "Amazing Grace," and "Motherless Child" with songs by such renowned gospel-spreaders as Waits and the Rolling Stones. Just as Cash believed he had his own personal Jesus, the Blind Boys of Alabama really do think Jesus is on his way back. For his part, Waits uses religious imagery in many of his songs. A few years after his "Jesus Gonna Be Here" came out, for example, "Chocolate Jesus" arrived on *Mule Variations*. Whatever he might believe, and no matter how often he mentions saints and sinners, his songs when he performs them do not feel religious the way they do when the Blind Boys of Alabama belt them out.

For a secularist, the concept of sin is invariably suspect, if not absurd, but the term as it is used in many god songs can be taken simply as a synonym for "wrong." You do not need a god to know when you have done something you should not have, to crave forgiveness from whomever you have mistreated, and to feel redeemed if you receive it. When King Lear says he is more sinned against than sinning, he acknowledges his own faults while simultaneously insisting he does not deserve the treatment he has received. Similarly, the denunciations of rambling, gambling and back-biting depicted in many a god song can be heard the same way, free of theological dimensions. The reality of the wrong is the pain it caused other people or that other people have caused the singer. The accounts of sorrow over actual human suffering, not violation of god-given rules, breathe life into songs about sinners.

While Cash may have recorded a selection of his mother's preferred hymns toward the end of his career, and recorded enough traditional gospel works to fill several albums over the course of his life, he also had plenty of sinner songs in his repertoire, including many about murder, often told from the perspective of the killer. "I shot a man in Reno / Just to watch him die," Cash sings in one of them. It may not be fully accurate to say of Cash, as William Blake said of John Milton, that he was "on the devil's side without knowing it," but Cash's records do reveal an ongoing interest in the activities of those who joined the fallen angel's party. (He might have called himself a former member of that group, in reference to his battles with drug addiction, though he did not stop singing about sin until death silenced him.) The songs also evince an awareness that, just as many readers find the Satan of *Paradise Lost* more interesting than the God, many listeners want to hear about people who do wrong, who are often more compelling than the upright and the holy. Those on the dark side live life with more verve. Part of what attracts performers and listeners to such songs is recognition. We identify with the sinner, who, in many country songs, serves as an anti-establishment figure. Of those first-person killer songs compiled on a disc simply named *Murder*, Cash noted: "We, the people, put ourselves in the shoes of the singer. We want to feel his pain, his loneliness. We want to be part of that rebellion." ("Better to reign in hell than serve in heaven," he might have added, with a nod toward Milton.) The songs offer even the true believer the vicarious thrill of sin. (For what it's worth, as of this writing, I've seen Mavis Staples perform live twice – once as part of a holiday program, once not – and both times her set spotlighted the sensual as well as the spiritual.)

Indulging in such flirting with the devil can be permitted among singers of god songs as long as it is accompanied elsewhere with the search for redemption and atonement for oneself – or punishment for persistent, unrepentant sinners. When I am the transgressor, these songs suggest, I thank God for his willingness to forgive, but when others do wrong, I relish the Almighty's willingness to show his wrath. (Take, for example, Julia Ward Howe's "Battle Hymn of the Republic": "He hath loosed the fateful lightning of His terrible swift sword.") Religious wishful thinking can be self-important; it can also be cruel. The joy felt for God's kindness or direct, individually tailored support somehow does not preclude a bloody minded pleasure when God denies others the warmth of his smile, when he cuts down those without pure religion. If you really subscribe to this sort of thinking, then I imagine it requires elaborate mental contortions to reconcile all these conflicting (though admittedly human) impulses. If you do not believe, then you can simply enjoy all the sinners' stories. They do get the great lines, just like in Milton's work.

The man alternately called the Reverend Gary Davis and Blind Gary Davis sang sermons in the style of the blues, some of which involve the thirst for righteous vengeance. Blind Willie Johnson recorded a song that Davis later made his own. It appears with eleven other vigorous god songs of complete conviction on *Harlem Street Singer,* which Davis recorded, alone with his guitar, in 1960. Davis called his telling of a biblical tale "Samson and Delilah," but Johnson gave his a title that spells out the song's expression of revenge-seeking anger that an atheist can appreciate regardless of its scriptural basis: "If I Had My Way I'd Tear that Building Down." The line forms the chorus. The song feels especially suitable for those days when God is not smiling down on you.

SECOND INTERLUDE

If true holidays feature respites from labor, then numerous second-class not-quite-holidays dot the calendar. They usually have entrenched holiday-like rituals and traditions (often aimed at encouraging commerce). Some have a civic or seasonal rather than religious nature. In the United States, there are several of them, including Groundhog Day and Flag Day.

These don't quite qualify as authentic holidays, but there's an intermediate class of near-holidays that might not involve breaks from school or work but do inflict obligations and particular forms of observations. Valentine's Day stands out among this group – and it doesn't stand apart from religion.

People might not know what to do on Martin Luther King Day but there's no confusion about what's expected on February 14th.

Of course, this doesn't mean people ought to do what they routinely do then ...

SIR SALMAN'S DAY

I.

"On St. Valentine's Day, 1989, the last day of her life..."

– The Ground Beneath Her Feet

Both for his unflagging love of literature despite those who would annihilate him because of it and for his undiminished faith in the possibility of love between individuals despite his knowledge of its fragility, Salman Rushdie could be seen as embodying Valentine's Day values. While that certainly beats being the lifeless testament to the persistence of superstitious barbarism that he almost became, it still leaves him saddled with an unfortunate symbolic burden.

It was on February 14, 1989, that Iran's Ayatollah Ruhollah Khomeini announced the infamous *fatwa* denouncing the author of *The Satanic Verses* (1988) and encouraging the faithful to slaughter him. While Rushdie lived in hiding, several serious attempts were made to carry out Khomeini's call, according to Scotland Yard. The pursuit of his death for an act of imagination attracted plenty of attention at the time, but Rushdie subsequently added more to his eventful Valentine's Day story. In a novel published a decade later, he imagined a character's death on the same date. While works of fiction shouldn't – can't – be read for reliable information about their authors, Rushdie's use of that pivotal day in *The Ground Beneath Her Feet* (1999) at least indicates it was still very much on his mind. Also on the tenth anniversary of receiving his "unfunny Valentine," Rushdie in a *New York Times* column reflected more directly on the effect the edict had on him: Life can be harsh, and for a decade St. Valentine's Day has reminded me of that harshness. But these dark anniversaries of the appalling Valentine I was sent in 1989 have also been times to reflect upon the countervailing value of love. Love feels more and more like the only subject.

Rushdie describes his response as a writer and proclaims his intensified commitment to the art of literature. Defending uninhibited creativity by exercising it amounts to an assertion of love in defiance of hateful dogma, Rushdie says. In the same piece, he reports feeling cleft in two with one Rushdie forever associated with the *fatwa* and the other simply trying to get on with writing books. These two, Rushdie the symbol and Rushdie the individual, can't cohabitate in comfort. The spokesperson for literary freedom at times overshadows the writer. Unable to ignore the "dire business" thrust upon him, he addressed it in articles and speeches, but worried that he risked "deafening the world to those other utterances, [his] books," and helped "to conceal the real Salman behind the smoky, sulfurous Rushdie of the Affair."

The story of the Rushdie Affair has as a subplot the pitiful group that suggested Rushdie invited his difficulties by daring to tell a tale in which Muhammad appears as part of a madman's dream. Members of this cowering tribe of extremism excusers tried to present him as a rude blasphemer who offended a fine old religion. John Cardinal O'Connor, the Archbishop of New York, agreed with Rushdie's would-be executioners that his novel was blasphemous and offensive. Writers who should have known better denounced not the bounty-promiser and -hunters but a colleague with a price on his head. John Le Carré, for instance, explained that all people are not "required to exhibit the same tolerance when their god is mocked" and that Rushdie consequently participated in "his own downfall." Rushdie "knew what he was doing and he cannot plead otherwise," opined Roald Dahl, who said that what Rushdie really was doing was aiming for the best-seller list. Graham Greene sympathized with the book burners, though he didn't believe Rushdie's "shocking bad taste" warranted his death. Whichever way he became perceived – hero or heel – Rushdie reasonably worried that his public role as an emblem diverted notice from his essential self's most meaningful efforts.

On the same symbolic date five years later, Rushdie added another chapter when he sought to align himself more intimately with "the only subject." On February, 14, 2004, he announced his engagement to model and television personality Padma Lakshmi. If on the tenth anniversary he reacted as a professional author, on the fifteenth he acted in a more personal way. If earlier statements dealt with abstractions, the pledge to marry amounted to a very particular expression of love. "To an ordinary human being," George Orwell observes, "love means nothing if it does not mean loving some people more than others." By declaring his love for one woman more than any others, Rushdie, I think, tried to became a regular person rather than the divisive and divided figure of the Rushdie Affair.

Indeed, by rejecting meddlesome, illegitimate authority and endorsing loving instead of fighting, Rushdie could be said to represent the best of Valentine's Day. One account of its origin claims a third-century Roman priest performed illegal marriages, violating a decree of emperor Claudius II, who preferred to keep young men single and therefore, he believed, more suitable soldier material. (Another account says the holiday was thrust upon an older Roman pagan feast – something of a Christian tradition that.)

The union between Rushdie and his fourth wife lasted only a few years; divorce proceedings began before the other, more ominous anniversary reached another divisible-by-five stage, but this doesn't sully the intent of Rushdie's gesture. Loving some people more than others doesn't always translate into loving them – or being loved by them – unceasingly, and the unwillingness to give up on marriage despite having experienced its failure suggests an admirably undaunted romantic temperament. (In his 2012 memoir *Joseph Anton*, in which he describes life under the *fatwa* as well as his serial marriages, Rushdie confirms this assessment. Regarding Lakshmi he has mostly sour things to say, but in connection with an earlier spouse he reflects: "that love could die did not mean it had not lived." The ability to love can survive even if a particular marriage can't.)

Though Rushdie might have become the most famous modern near-martyr for the art of fiction (and it shouldn't be forgotten that several people associated with *The Satanic Verses* were physically attacked and one of its translators was murdered), he is not alone in his efforts to salvage something of the day's spirit of rebellion against despots determined to flex the muscles of their detestation. Saw Wai, for instance, sought to wed expressions of love with protest. The Burmese poet was arrested in January 2008 after one of his poems, with an imbedded denunciation of the ruling dictator, appeared in print. Described by the Associated Press as the author of "innocuous love poems for Burmese-language magazines and journals," Saw Wai structured his "February 14" so that if read vertically the first word of each line formed the following: "Power crazy Senior General Than Shwe." (The name of military junta's head contains the Burmese words for "million" and "gold," which the poet found ways to incorporate into his verse on the meaning of love.) After the writer's detention, copies of the magazine that published his poem were removed from newsstands in Rangoon.

People who routinely endure the sort of tyranny that spawned the threat to Rushdie's existence have emphasized the importance of individuals' personal preferences, just as he tried to fifteen years after the *fatwa*, by celebrating Valentine's Day where doing so is explicitly forbidden. In Saudi Arabia, the Commission for the Promotion of Virtue and Prevention of Vice declared it a "pagan feast" and, in February 2007, the institution that enforces the Wahhabi version of Islamic religious doctrine (the *mutawwa*) announced that it "would systematically inspect hotels, restaurants, coffeehouses, and gift shops to prevent Muslim couples from giving each other Valentines or other presents," according to journalist Stephen Schwartz and Irfan al-Alawi, director of the Islamic Heritage Research Foundation. However, "Saudi subjects report that the *mutawwa* harassment failed. Many ordinary Saudi Muslims favored their beloved with Valentines gifts, which were more popular than ever." Schwartz and al-Alawi see this as a possible hint of a "movement away from tyranny." They write: "If a serious Valentine Revolution were to develop in the Saudi kingdom, its success would have incalculably beneficial effects in the Muslim world, undermining the appeal of Wahhabism and curbing the cash flow to al Qaeda, contributing to regional stability, and providing a responsible alternative to the demagogy of [Iranian president Mahmoud] Ahmadinejad and others."

Sending a Valentine isn't personal, then; it's political. If by exchanging signs of love individuals challenge rigid social control by religious rulers, then Rushdie's announcement of his wedding plans on Valentine's Day left him no less of a symbolic warrior in the fight against violent fundamentalism than he had been earlier. Schwartz and al-Alawi are unduly optimistic about the sharpness of red roses' subversive thorns. After all, even in the legend associated with the day, Saint Valentine's secret marriages didn't bring about the downfall of the Roman Empire, and, in the real world, Saw Wai's poetic assault toppled neither Than Shwe's military organization (the Tatmadaw) nor the ruling regime (the State Peace and Development Council, the outfit formerly and more sinisterly known as the State Law and Order Restoration Council, or SLORC). Nonetheless, by insisting on the day's implications in the public realm, they complicate Rushdie's efforts to close the rift Khomeini opened and might actually widen it instead. Put another way, even if Rushdie aimed to make the sort of personal, individual romantic gesture expected of regular people (in some parts of the world) on Valentine's Day, the holiday's political component meant he still remained a combatant in the coliseum of symbolism.

II.

"Now it's noon on Valentine's Day. We have been here before."

– The Ground Beneath Her Feet

Valentine's Day 1989 started a new phase in an old confrontation, and even Rushdie's friend Christopher Hitchens couldn't help but think of him in terms of war rather than love. Writing about the twentieth anniversary of what he calls "the single worst review any novelist has ever had," Hitchens conceded that events engulfing *The Satanic Verses* make it all too easy to overlook Rushdie's "humorous and ironic side." That's what Hitchens would have preferred to write about – Rushdie the individual, Rushdie the writer – but he couldn't help returning to Rushdie the symbol. The furor over Rushdie's novel, Hitchens believed, spread strife between those who would impose religious law and those who resist it out of the Muslim world and into the West. "For our time and generation," Hitchens wrote, "the great conflict between the ironic mind and the literal mind, the experimental and the dogmatic, the tolerant and the fanatical, is the argument that was kindled by *The Satanic Verses*." Rushdie might prefer to see himself as a descendant of Joaquim Maria Machado de Assis, Miguel de Cervantes, Nikolai Gogol, Franz Kafka, Herman Melville and others forming his "polyglot family tree," but Hitchens traced his lineage in a different tradition. "Almost every historic battle for free expression, from Socrates to Galileo," he claimed, "has begun as a struggle over what is and is not 'blasphemy.'"

Among the perverse outcomes of this struggle were not only incidents of overt censorship, as with the pulping of Saw Wai's poem, but also tremulous self-censorship. The very right Rushdie sought to keep strong by using it, the media let atrophy in order to avoid the blasphemy tag. Events involving other depictions of the same character Rushdie writes about in The Satanic Verses illustrate the point. In September 2005, the Danish newspaper *Jyllands-Posten* printed a dozen cartoons of Muhammad. Several months later, Muslim rioters responded to the "blasphemous" drawings by burning and vandalizing Danish embassies in the Middle East and Africa, which resulted in approximately 200 deaths. An ax- and knife-wielding man linked with a Muslim group broke into the home of one of the cartoonists. Four years after the original appearance of the cartoons (which major American television networks, newspapers and magazines refused to show in reports about the furious reaction to them), a U.S. academic publisher decided not to include them, or other depictions of the prophet by artists like Sandro Botticelli and Salvador Dalí, in a scholarly study of the controversy. Yale University Press decided to drop the very images Jytte Klausen writes about in *The Cartoons that Shook the World* (2009). Its director, John Donatich, said he didn't want "blood on [his] hands," as if the targets of it, rather than the religious fanatics who commit it, would be responsible for any potential violence. In *Joseph Anton*, Rushdie cites the publisher's move as one of several examples of the "climate of fear" that make it more difficult for books like *The Satanic Verses* to be published, "or even, perhaps, to be written." His survival and the continued availability of his novel, he says, don't mean the battle ended in victory for free speech and free thought.

When Iran declared Rushdie deserving of capital punishment for the ancient thought crime, it lit a fuse that continued to burn even after the country backed away from the *fatwa* in 1998. When, in 2007, the British government named Rushdie a knight, Iran declared Islam insulted once again. Pakistan amplified the whine of offense. "This is a source of anguish for Muslims, and it will encourage people to commit blasphemy against Prophet Mohammad," said Sher Afghan Niazi, Pakistan's Minister for Parliamentary Affairs. Although he denied endorsing suicide murder in retaliation, Pakistan's Minister for Religious Affairs nonetheless blamed Rushdie and his lionizers in advance for any violence committed by upset Muslims. "We have to look at the root causes of militancy," Ijaz ul Haq said. "The root cause is that you are giving knighthood to someone who commits blasphemy. This leads to extremism and there is a danger of people considering suicide attacks in retaliation." Eighteen years after an Iranian leader called for the execution of the non-Iranian Rushdie, representatives of Pakistan's government demanded Britain reverse its decision to honor the non-Pakistani Rushdie for his contribution to literature. According to *The Guardian,* protesters in Pakistan joined the Khomeini school of literary criticism by burning effigies of Rushdie and chanting, "Kill him! Kill him!" Such renewed calls for the obliteration of a novelist should spur the non-dogmatic to feel outrage, I'd say.

As with the Danish cartoons, Rushdie's knighthood didn't only bother Muslims in predominantly Muslim countries. Dr. Muhammad Abdul Bari, secretary general of the Muslim Council of Britain, called it "insensitive" and complained of the hurt feelings blasphemy causes. "Salman Rushdie earned notoriety among Muslims for the highly insulting and blasphemous manner in which he portrayed early Islamic figures much-loved and honored by them." Performing the same sort of intellectual gymnastics that result in blaming those on the receiving end for the violence directed at them, Labor peer Lord Ahmed declared that Rushdie, "a man who has insulted the British public and been divisive in community relations," had – that phrase again – "blood on his hands." The novelist, not the vengeful Islamist, is the problem, you see.

Given his personal history, Rushdie might have sought to distance himself from the day named for a saint that may have arisen to commemorate surreptitious religious ceremonies. "When murder is ordered in the name of god you begin to think less well of the name of god," he remarked four years after his murder was ordered in the name of God. "Religion is the poison in the blood," Rushdie contends, and envisioning the hearts pumping it as red foil-covered chocolates or lace-fringed construction paper cutouts doesn't change that. In practice, of course, Valentine's Day has virtually nothing to do with religion, but that doesn't remove the inarguable reasons for wariness of it.

III.

"...she wouldn't have been in Mexico on that fateful Valentine's Day, so she'd still be alive."

– The Ground Beneath Her Feet

Nonetheless, Rushdie, like those irrepressible Saudi Arabian celebrants, refused to sit it out. In the United States – where the peripatetic India-born, Cambridge-educated writer eventually decided to live – most people join in. Indeed, far from having even a hint of rebelliousness, Valentine's Day American-style encourages conformity, and most people do not resist the subtle and not-so-subtle societal pressure to trade semi-mandatory declarations of devotion via commercial transactions. Approximately two-thirds of American households exchange Valentines, according to the Census

Bureau; only Christmas sees more greeting cards given. Declining to observe the pseudo-holiday invites suspicions that you're a cold, unfeeling miser unwilling to bestow a small token of affection on your poor, unappreciated partner. Consequently, buying presents or dining out on the designated day, rather than demonstrating passion, may amount to no more than meeting expectations. I've heard of elementary schools reducing the ritual to a senseless muddle by disregarding the fundamental truth of human love and calibrating Valentine's Day festivities so all pupils give and receive cards. Just as sensitive religious souls beg to be shielded from insult or offense, school children evidently must be protected from their peers' self-esteem-ravaging indifference. Charlie Brown must get Valentines, even if assigning the Little Red-Haired Girl and other classmates to dispense them violates the spirit of the red-letter day and inculcates insincerity by mandating expressions of unfelt affection.

Rushdie the writer did take love, truly felt love, as his principal subject, and in his work romantic ardor and imagination intertwine as constitutive elements of what it is to be human. "All men needed to hear their stories told," he writes in *The Enchantress of Florence* (2008). A character called, among other names, the Mughal of Love worries about suffering the "intolerable" end of dying without telling his tale. "He was a man, but if he died without telling the story he would be something less that that, an albino cockroach, a louse." He does survive to tell it to a man who has multiple flesh-and-blood wives but who favors one he conjures in his mind. In *Shalimar the Clown* (2005), Rushdie restages *Romeo and Juliet* in a Kashmiri village where teenagers Boonyi and Shalimar fall in love and marry. She's from a Hindu family, he a Muslim. As that scenario might immediately suggest, love and violence share close quarters. Intimating his future incarnation as an assassin, Shalimar tells Boonyi he'll kill her if she ever leaves him. "What a romantic you are," she replies. Fans of singer Vina Aspara, the Valentine's Day victim of *The*

Ground Beneath Her Feet, believe her former bandmate and lover is responsible. "[Y]ou fucking murderer, Ormus Cama, don't think we will ever forget or forgive," the hate mail reads.

By figuratively responding to his hate mail by sending a single Valentine to Lakshmi, Rushdie added romantic love to the literary love he'd proclaimed in previous Februaries. His bid to assert his individual self on February 14 didn't end its association with his representative self, however; instead, it affiliated him not only with the finest of the day's traditions but with all of them. Given Rushdie's harrowing Valentine's Day experiences, consideration of him in connection with the holiday's comparatively minor and mild coercive aspects might seem trivializing, I know. Given that rabid zealots started howling for his blood on Valentine's Day, does it really matter that on the same date millions of English speakers – almost all of them lacking his astonishing facility with the language – buy sweets and flowers for each other out of a sense of obligation? For the sake of Rushdie the writer I believe it does. Just as it's understandable that in his fiction Rushdie has love, creativity and death as well as Valentine's Day itself intersect and intermingle, it's easy to see why he might try to reclaim control over his own story from those who want to write its ending. In his version, Valentine's Day would not be the last day of his life; it would be the beginning of a new life with a new wife. As an author Rushdie ebulliently combines history and literature in prose of unrivaled exuberance, but as a man revealing his plans to marry, he settled for the romantic equivalent of something he energetically avoids in his work: a cliché. Despite what his most vociferous critics contend and that one distracting day can obscure, Rushdie really does realize his best self in his books.

THIRD INTERLUDE

The famously upbeat Philip Larkin may have been referring to parents when he said they fuck you up unintentionally – I don't expect ever to see his poem "This Be the Verse" reprinted in a Mother's Day or Father's Day card – but he could have been writing about teachers, who can also pass along plenty of misery. Indeed, some deliberately try to fill you with faults.

Then again, just like mum and dad, teachers can impart lessons very different from what they intend, and consequently be quite helpful and liberating. As Rushdie writes in Joseph Anton: *"The lessons one learns at school are not always the ones the school thinks it's teaching." Sometimes you can learn despite what they try to teach you – even on days off.*

HOLLOW EGGS AND SEEDS OF DOUBT

I.

"... death,
The undiscovered country from whose bourn
No traveller returns..."

– Hamlet, 3.1.80-82

Father P. was a strange man, and not only because he was a priest. Using broad-tipped magic markers, he would copy sentences from the novels we studied onto colorful construction paper and hang the signs above the blackboard on the painted cinderblock walls of his classroom. Over the course of a semester, the hand-made posters would change frequently in the space they shared with the ever-present American flag and crucifix. He slicked his oily hair straight back, and sometimes he would run a comb through it during a lecture. The hairstyle emphasized the largeness of his jowly face, which looked something like the worn, weary and bloated visage of the older Marlon Brando, whose voice my high school English teacher's also resembled. Imagine reading Conrad with Colonel Kurtz.

Quirks of personal appearance or unique pedagogical techniques did not distinguish him from his peers. These included the avowed celibate who mustered the temerity to take on a class called Marriage and Family. Even his co-religionist pupils strained to suppress their laughter when the great yawning gulf between his subject and his qualifications to teach it showed itself, as it inevitably did. (Father P. could at least legitimately claim to know firsthand the literary material he taught.) Father P.'s coworker bizarrely, memorably and misogynistically compared trying sexual intercourse with a less-than-fully erect penis to inserting cooked spaghetti into a pencil sharpener. His attempts at worldly humor included an explanation why we should never call female human beings, none of whom occupied desks beside us, "dolls" (because dolls have heads filled with sawdust and can be laid anywhere). When teaching psychology, a certain priest felt compelled to confess his alcoholism, something of an occupational hazard among his fellow collar-wearers, I learned. Another one would bribe students to stay and talk with him in counseling sessions, which were mandatory but of unspecified length, by freely dispensing otherwise forbidden cigarettes.

Instead, what set Father P. apart from his colleagues was his evident willingness to accept that pupils could be intelligent and thoughtful and *not* share the views of the Catholic Church. Unlike other teachers, he made no effort to promote the institutional line. While most of the other instructors told students what to believe, Father P. seemed sincerely to want his students to think – actively, critically, rigorously – and not merely accept as true what they heard or read. He knew I did not come from a Catholic family. He could see from my efforts to test the limits of the school's dress code that I had a healthy teenage disrespect for authority. I put in my time in detention, which the school doled by the JUG (*i.e.*, justice under God). He probably heard from his professional and confessional brethren that I liked to challenge the ideas promulgated in the required religion courses. After one class, he pulled me aside to tell me that it was good to ask questions and that I should keep it up. I found it odd at the time. I don't think I even raised my hand that day in the room bearing his personal decorative stamp. Later I realized that he referred not to anything I said in that particular session. Rather, he wanted to assure me that he approved of my skepticism *in general.* It was not at all typical for a priest in a Jesuit high school to endorse a nonbeliever's nonbelief in this way.

I think of Father P. when I try to understand why people continue to have faith. I suspect he was struggling with his own. His encouraging comment to me means little on its own, but I wonder if he didn't offer other signs too. The list of books he assigned did not vary much from one year to the next. Younger students could expect to read the same works older students did in previous years. One year, however, he decided to take a break from *A Portrait of the Artist as a Young Man* and taught *Eric* in its usual place. I remember him saying that the mark of a true classic was its ability to endure, but I doubt he truly believed James Joyce and Doris Lund approached similar heights of literary greatness. When I learned that Father P. died of cancer a few years after I graduated, I could not help but speculate that his health had something to do with our reading a mother's account of her son's leukemia. I wondered if his own cancer and attendant reflections on mortality had shaken his certainty of eternal life via belief in the divinity of Jesus. (In 2011, an online community called the Clergy Project was created precisely so that active and former clergy who'd abandoned supernatural beliefs could discuss such developments. In its first two years, it attracted hundreds of members.) Did he see in me, someone who rejected such faith, an open asker of questions that he could no longer confidently answer in his own mind? Did he recognize the doubter he was becoming?

II.

"Apart from personal vanity, it is clearly fear of death that causes the persistent belief in a future life, despite all indications to the contrary."

– Ibn Warraq

The fear of death readily perceptible behind stories like the Easter tale certainly spurs many to adhere to a fantastical conviction of a cosmic reprieve. Who wouldn't want his death sentence commuted? One way to cope with the frightening idea of oblivion is to deny its reality, to pretend we do not die or that death is not really the end that it so convincingly appears to be. We don't really die, see, we come back, like He did, because He did, on the Sunday after Good Friday.

Wanting something to be true does not make it so, of course, and the Bible offers plenty of reasons to dismiss its promise of circumventing the stark finality of death. Its pivotal resurrection story collapses under even casual scrutiny. John's version of the death and resurrection of Jesus includes elements not in the gospels according to Matthew, Mark or Luke. He has the scene involving the character known as doubting Thomas, which he uses to present the pernicious notion that faith is superior to belief based on evidence. John depicts Jesus as having "manifested to his disciples" three times "after he was risen from the dead" (21.14). Thomas missed the first one and did not believe what he heard about it. He wanted to see the nail holes in Jesus' hands and the wound from where a soldier pierced his side (20.25) – something that exclusively occurs in John's telling of the tale (19.34), by the way. When, a little over a week later, Jesus again saunters onto the scene, he permits Thomas's examination of his body, which convinces Thomas that his lord and god has indeed returned. After show and tell, Jesus says to him: "Because thou hast seen me, Thomas, thou hast believed: blessed are they that have not seen, and have believed" (20.29). Thomas, understandably enough, had boldly questioned the veracity of those who said a man who died then revived. Jesus scolds temerarious Thomas for his faithlessness. It would have been better – *he* would have been better – if he had abandoned all critical faculties and just swallowed the incredible story he was told.

This is just one of multiple transparent tactics John uses to shield his writing from skeptics who might demand proof of its reliability. These maneuvers end up conflicting with each other. In addition to asserting the moral superiority of unthinking faith over legitimate doubt, he invokes the claims to trustworthiness of an eye-witness account, even though *not* seeing is believing. In other words, seeing counts sometimes, but not when simply believing is in order. In the end, though, John just demands you take him at his word. After describing blood and water pouring from Jesus' spear-perforated side, John writes, "And he that saw it, hath given testimony; and his testimony is true. And he knoweth that he saith true, that you also may believe" (19.35). Not convinced? John also holds out the promise of a reward for believing what he has written. More than once he concedes that he has not prepared an exhaustive history of Jesus' life, but he insists that he has written enough "that you may believe that Jesus is the Christ, the Son of God: and that believing, may have life in his name" (20.31). Eternal life depends on taking John at his word. He ends his gospel by claiming that there simply is not enough space to record everything Jesus did (21.25). Frankly, I cannot imagine Father P. ever having accepted a book report that made wild claims with no supporting evidence and instead stated that, first of all, evidence ought not to be needed and, second, I tell you it's true and you should therefore trust me, and, finally, I just did not have room to include it all. Yet at some point in his life he bought the book to which John and the others contributed, whatever doubts I began to imagine he might have eventually formed.

John is not alone in demanding belief in the resurrection of Jesus in order to beat death. In Mark's account, Mary Magdalen meets with disbelief when she tells Jesus' male followers that she visited his grave and learned that he was alive. Later, Jesus "appeared in another shape to two of them," who tell their unbelieving associates about what they saw. Finally, Jesus showed up and "upbraided them with their incredulity and hardness of heart, because they did not believe them who had seen him after he was risen again" (16.14). He proceeds to inform them that salvation requires both belief and baptism, while unbelief results in condemnation (16.16).

Luke also has the apostles initially disbelieving "idle tales" of Jesus' return (24.11). Unlike John's Jesus, Luke's Son of God has no problem at all with people scrutinizing his hands and feet. John has Jesus tell Mary Magdalen not to touch him because he has "not yet ascended to [his] Father" (John 20.17) – as if she could touch him then – but Luke's Jesus invites his followers to "handle" his "flesh and bones" (Luke 24.39). His corporeal Jesus not only allows physical contact, he also requests food (Luke 24.41). While in Luke satiated Jesus gives the uneaten remains to his disciples, John has a more convivial Jesus invite the apostles to dine with him (John 21.12). Matthew and Mark stay silent concerning any post-resurrection meal or postprandial dispersal of leftovers.

Many other discrepancies separate the four stories of Jesus' final act from each other and from factuality. All put a version of the sign designating Jesus as "King of the Jews" atop his cross (Matthew 27.37, Mark 16.26, Luke 23.28, John 19.19-20), but only Luke and John specify convenient presentation of the title in Greek, Latin and Hebrew. This minor variation, a mere detail, does not make the stories irreconcilable, but other differences do. Matthew claims the earth quaked when Jesus died (27.51) and says another earthquake coincided with the removal of the stone sealing the sepulcher where his body was briefly stored. The other three say nothing of such noteworthy phenomena. Matthew places one angel inside the sepulcher to explain the absence of Jesus' earthly leavings (28.2). Mark assigns the task to one man (16.5). Luke puts two men in the cave (24.4). John cranks it up a heavenly notch by seating a pair of angels where the corpse had been (20.12). The gospels have different tallies of how many women were at the tomb that Sunday morning – one, two, three and more than four. John not only includes uncertain Thomas; he also has nailed-up Jesus talk down from the cross to his mother, an episode the others fail to mention (John 19.25-26). While Matthew, Mark and John have Pontius Pilate agreeing to the crucifixion, Luke alone involves Herod in Jesus' final terrestrial reckoning. (Luke is also the only one to have Jesus speak the condescending and – given that his death purportedly forms a key part of a larger plan – nonsensical line, "Father, forgive them, for they know not what they do" [23.34].)

Obviously the good-news quartet cannot all tell literally true versions of the tale. Either Pilate was the sole official of Galilee to okay the death sentence for Jesus or he was not. Jesus either happily showed off his scars or grew petulant when someone asked to see them. He chatted with his mother or he didn't. One or two figures, of this world or not, could have provided a reason for Jesus' body disappearing a few days after his death. His resurrection might qualify as planet wobbling, metaphorically speaking, but if seismic shifting actually happened, it certainly counts as peculiar that most chroniclers don't mention it.

Matthew, Mark, Luke and John don't only differ in their accounts of the end of Jesus' life; they also diverge when documenting its start. To begin with, only two of the four cover the nativity scene, and Matthew and Luke disagree on a number of basic points. The former says Joseph and Mary lived in Bethlehem and later moved to Nazareth. The latter says they had been long-term Nazareth residents and were in Bethlehem for a Roman census for which there is no historical record and ample reason to believe didn't occur. Matthew says wise men were present, Luke says shepherds, and neither has both constituencies represented. Matthew has a star in the East; Luke doesn't mention it, though he does have singing angels, which Matthew leaves out. They can't agree on Jesus' lineage either, though both try to connect him to King David. Matthew lists twenty-eight generations between David and Jesus. Luke lists forty-one. The pair proposes different names for Joseph's father and grandfather. They give different names for each ancestor separating Joseph from Zorobabel, another Old Testament character. Incredibly, for the 500-year span preceding the birth of Jesus, the supposedly divinely-inspired evangelists can't agree on the name of a single one of Joseph's forebears. Then again, if his mother was a virgin, his human stepfather's genealogy hardly matters anyway.

The Bible's many contradictions have been scrupulously documented by others willing to take the time. In *Self-contradictions of the Bible* (1860), William Henry Burr delineates 144 propositions, both historical and theological, that the book presents and undermines. Writer Tom Flynn compared and contrasted the incompatible family trees drawn up by Matthew and Luke. Sam Harris observes in *The End of Faith* (2004) that the Bible overflows with passages that "represent perfect contradictions (that is, one cannot affirm the truth of one without equally asserting the falsity of the other)." For him, the book's inconsistencies drastically diminish its worth:

There is, perhaps, no greater evidence for the imperfection of the Bible as an account of reality, divine or mundane, than such instances of self-refutation. Of course, once faith has begun its reign of folly, even perfect contradictions may be relished as heavenly rebukes to earthly logic. Martin Luther closed the door on reason with a single line: "The Holy Spirit has an eye only to substance and is not bound by words." The Holy Spirit, it seems, is happy to play tennis without the net.

I merely mention a few examples related to certain incidents, but the lack of agreement among the gospels typifies the book as a whole.

Even decades after my years in Catholic school, Ash Wednesday, when people deliberately walk around with dirt smeared on their foreheads as if it were a reasonable thing to do, still startles me. I don't intentionally walk about with a dirty face; I have no use for a crude sign of unwillingness to accept death's inevitability. After Ash Wednesday (and barring any explosive illustrations of faithful fanaticism) my bafflement at otherwise sane people's credulity and eagerness to submit to supernatural nonsense usually rests until Easter reawakens it several weeks later – it's one of those cyclical things.

III.

"An individual who should survive his physical death is also beyond my comprehension, nor do I wish it otherwise; such notions are for the fears or absurd egoism of feeble souls."

– Albert Einstein

More striking, to me, than biblical incongruity is the insipidness of the risen Jesus. He didn't die for our sins. He overslept for them. He returns, in essence, to say, "See, it's me." He tells the apostles that they should believe, as should others who never see him. John shows him giving tips for effective fishing (21.6). The teacher shows up to say his teachings should continue to be taught. If his moral guidance has merit, of course, it ought to survive regardless of whether he returned from the dead to say so. Or, to paraphrase something Kurt Vonnegut's grandfather said to him, if what Jesus said was good, and some of it was, then it doesn't matter whether he was God. (Some of it wasn't so good though, as when declares that he did *not* come to promote peace on earth but came instead to wield a sword [Matthew 10.34], and that anyone who failed to abide him would be cast into flames [John 15.6].)

Just as wishful thinking fails to make stories of death's defeat true, it also cannot will them into to being sensible or even good. The scriptural rationale for the death of Jesus is convoluted and ultimately absurd:

> For God so loved the world, that he gave his only begotten Son, that whosoever believeth in him should not perish, but have everlasting life. For God sent not his Son into the world to condemn the world; but that the world through him might be saved. He that believeth on him is not condemned: but he that believeth not is condemned already, because he hath not believed in the name of the only begotten Son of God. (John 3.16-18)

The deal works something like this: God shows his love – love for those whom the faithful like to call God's children – by sending his sole child to be killed. *If* you believe this, then you get eternal life, which you get to spend with a jealous God who will condemn those who fail to believe. ("He that believeth on the Son hath everlasting life: and he that believeth not the Son shall not see life; but the wrath of God abideth on him," writes John [3.36], who also relies on the rhetorical tactic of frequent repetition.) This is the same supreme being, recall, who set up the whole arrangement in the first place, including making people mortal, which they are not, if (and only if) they believe in Him and willfully ignore the reality of the grave. And if they believe that sending offspring to death demonstrates love for the world and that such a sacrifice shows that death is not final. And, depending on which truth-teller they take as the most reliable, if they are baptized to boot. Passages like this make it impossible for me to regard the Bible as *a* let alone *the* good book (though I concede that "In the beginning God created heaven and earth" is not a bad opening line – for a children's tale).

While the fear of death may animate Easter's founding

myths, other emotional states also give rise to stories of the undead dead. Older imaginings of an afterlife have obvious connections with Christian conception of it, but instead of dramatizing dread over the inevitable disappearance of the self they confront the pain of losing relatives and friends. Homer and Virgil describe immortal souls that survive bodies' deaths. In *The Iliad*, Homer has a ghost of a former comrade visit Achilles to demand the proper disposal of his body so that the "Shades that are images of used-up men" will permit him to "pass the gates of death" (23.70-1). After agreeing to perform the required funeral rites, Achilles tries to embrace his former friend:

> He stretched his arms out but took hold of nothing,
> as into earth Patróklos' shade like smoke
> retreated with a faint cry. (23.101-3)

Both poets have heroes visit with departed parents. When Odysseus goes to the realm of Hades, he sees "the soul of [his] perished mother" (*The Odyssey*, 11.141). He wishes to hug her, but cannot:

> ...Three times
> I started toward her, and my heart was urgent to
> hold her,
> and three times she fluttered out of my hands like a
> shadow
> or a dream, and the sorrow sharpened at the heart
> within me... (11.205-208)

Writing several centuries later – but still before Matthew, Mark, Luke and John – Virgil echoes these lines in *The Aeneid* when Aeneas tries to embrace the immaterial remains of his father:

...Three times
he tried to throw his arms around Anchises'
neck; and three times the Shade escaped from that
vain clasp – like light winds, or most like
swift dreams. (6.924-927)

Aeneas inadvertently reveals the illogic of these visits to the underworld when he begs Dido to talk with him since, "This is the last time fate will let us speak" (6.614) – as if he is not going to die as well.

The older Greek and Roman stories of the living wanting to hug dead loved ones but finding that they cannot conveys a deeper emotional truth than the conflicting accounts of Jesus' promise of eternal life to anyone who believes in his post-crucifixion forays among his apostles. The resurrected Jesus theoretically could have been hugged – he came back with a body rather than as the mere "wisp of life" in "a visible" form that Achilles tried to touch (*The Iliad*, 23.105-6) – but no one seemed to think of it. It may have been when discussing Virgil, who so concisely captures the hurt of separation in the passage about Aeneas' "vain clasp," that Father P. pointed to longevity as a hallmark of literary excellence.

IV.

"Men live so briefly that their plans far outrun their ability to execute them. They see themselves cut off before their will to live is exhausted."

– Carl Van Doren

Literature, rife as it may be in afterlife fantasies, confronts competition in the comeback story market. Sports could not sustain their popularity if they didn't reliably provide narratives of the stunning turnaround and redemption in the form of the unexpected win: the boxer who wills himself off the canvas and goes on to win the fight, the runner who recovers from a stumble and retakes the lead, the three-point basket at the buzzer that puts the team ahead by one and so on. Often these stories appear to transcend the relatively insignificant realm of sport to point to some greater truth about perseverance and endurance: Lasse Viren falling in the 1972 Olympic 10,000 meter final but getting back on his feet to win the race in record time or Muhammad Ali reclaiming the heavyweight championship after having been stripped of his title and barred from boxing because of his refusal to enter the armed forces. Not coincidentally, the shade sightings in *The Iliad* and *The Aeneid* coincide with funeral games, suggesting that death predictably and perpetually spurs the living to turn to physical contests for reassurance of their continued vitality.

Bountiful nature itself supplies the substance for innumerable metaphors of rebirth and renewal. Spring festivals pre-date Christianity. In the Common Era, plenty of people disregard the theological angle and embrace Easter as a festival of spring, if for no other reason for the pleasure of tending to their gardens. What could provide a more perfect symbol of ceaseless, eternal return than the flowers and plants that come to life at that time of year? Well, perhaps eggs. In cynical moments I've wondered if cunning adults bestow hollow chocolate Easter eggs in order to teach children lessons about the risks of forming inflated expectations. Those colorfully wrapped confectionary false promises, even if not intended to prepare children for the inevitability of disappointment, regularly have that result when initially hopeful but immediately disillusioned recipients break them open and find nothing inside the thin crumbly shell. Reproduction via material parents – physical fathers and non-virginal mothers – offers the most genuine hope for any sort of victory over death. Of course, in non-metaphorical procreation it's the species that perpetuates itself, not individual members. As with those foil covered candy letdowns, something could be learned if people would only really look at what the symbols more precisely represent rather than searching for narrative ways to evade their fears.

One of the reasons that the Bible survives from one century to the next, despite its decidedly uneven literary merit, is because youngsters are encouraged to be faithful rather than critical and to believe what parents and teachers tell them rather than to read closely the venerated document. Atheist and agnostics tend to have better knowledge of the religions they reject than those professing belief, as documented in the Pew Forum on Religion and Public Life's 2010 U.S. Religious Knowledge Survey. Clergy, scholars and other fanatical cranks may really read the Bible, but typical believers just absorb (some of) what they are told. The only way I know to test this theory is to ask people whether they've actually looked at every page, and when I've done this most respondents admit they have not. However, I readily acknowledge that I don't run with a faithful crowd.

I also concede that evidence of my former literature instructor developing doubts when diagnosed with a terminal disease must be seen as slim. The Brando lookalike who assigned Graham Greene also had his students read, in *Eric*, about a man not ready to die forced to face his impending demise. No matter how Father P. may have tried to follow Jesus' example, he did not give the same advice to questioning Thomases. Although we never read *Of Human Bondage* in his class, I think the teacher, like Somerset Maugham's Philip Carey, realized that it "was evidently possible to be virtuous and unbelieving." Unlike Maugham's protagonist, I never thought I "was the creature of a God who appreciated the discomfort of his worshippers," so I never had to abandon such a belief. Yet I think that thoughtful people raised in such a tradition must at least contemplate rebelling against it at some point, even if they never come to Carey's position of being "thankful not to have to believe in God, for then such a condition of things would be intolerable; one could reconcile oneself to existence only because it was meaningless." Without question, many people, when they sense death's approach, take refuge from fear in faith, but at least some must start wondering, and wondering hard, whether to remain confident of a future post-death life. Viewing fatal illness as part of some divine design could also easily become hard to stomach even for those not undergoing chemotherapy.

I don't believe what I do because I find it comforting or reject ideas because I find them unpleasant, but I do not think this way because Father P. urged me to do so. Indeed, priests who discouraged questioning probably did more than he to spur me to seek evidence for what I believe and to be wary of those who do not. Despite all their efforts, the Jesuits ended up convincing me not to be cajoled into faith by a contradictory anthology of fanciful fictions and fiery enjoinders.

So I did end up learning something at Catholic school, even from those with a less subtle, nuanced and possibly worried mind than Father P.

FOURTH INTERLUDE

In mid-nineteenth-century New York City, a man named William Thompson stopped pedestrians and asked, "Have you confidence in me to trust me with your watch until to-morrow?" Anyone with such confidence found out within twenty-four hours that he would not get his timepiece back. Thompson's scheme not only prompted a New York Herald *reporter to coin the term "confidence man"; it also supplied Herman Melville with the idea for (and the title of) a novel,* The Confidence-Man: His Masquerade, *which was published in 1857 and baffled contemporary reviewers.*

Efforts to fool others, whether to relieve them of their belongings or merely for the sake of Candid Camera-*style fun, require ingenuity. The idea is to mislead people and have them willingly accede to sly propositions, to persuade them to trust and have confidence in liars. Without trickery, confidence games would amount to no more than thievery or coercion. True con-men do not resort to violence or the threat of it. Instead, they rely solely on what showman P.T. Barnum in his autobiography calls the "faculty of judiciously applying soft soap" and "the faculty to please and flatter the public so judiciously as not to have them suspect your intentions."*

Confidence men and their targets navigate a world in which not everyone is honest and not everything is as it appears. Thus, confidence games provided Melville with rich material because they entail questions of practical epistemology: Who can you trust? How do you know what information is reliable? And how can you use it to your advantage? Finding the balance between trusting without being a gullible dupe and remaining skeptical without becoming a cynical, hateful ogre, The Confidence-Man *suggests, is a fundamental human dilemma. If you im-*

mediately suspect the motives of someone who remarks, as one of Melville's characters does, "how much pleasanter to puff at this philanthropic pipe, than still to keep fumbling at that misanthropic rifle," sure that he aims to deprive you of your valuables, it's easy to develop the view of another Melville character, who believes "the human animal is ... a losing animal. Can't be trusted; less trustworthy than oxen; for conscientiousness a turn-spit dog excels him." Melville dramatizes the difficulty, perhaps even the impossibility, of capturing the elusive, cunning truth. He also satirizes those who believe they've already got a firm grasp on the capital-T Truth and need look no further.

Not coincidentally, the various exchanges comprising The Confidence-Man occur on April Fools' Day.

PARADE OF FOOLS

April Fools' Day's claim to fame, its reason for existing, is silly practical jokes. It may have been that for Herman Melville (whose humorous side is too often overlooked), but for him it surely was the right day to set a novel made up almost entirely of conversations in which one shipboard stranger toys with another's confident belief in, well, almost anything. *The Confidence-Man* features multiple tricksters (or serial manifestations by a shape-shifting, appearance-altering demon) playing various scams: a crippled beggar, a man down on his luck seeking a loan, a doctor selling cures, a charity agent soliciting donations and the like. "Melville's book now seems a prophetically postmodern work in which swindler cannot be distinguished from swindled and the confidence man tells truth and lies simultaneously," Andrew Delbanco writes in *Melville: His World and Work* (2005). The indeterminate nature of Melville's confidence man underlines the unlikelihood of arriving at certainty. "Is he, or is he not, what he seems to be?" a character asks. Melville does not offer a simple answer. "Looks are one thing, and facts are another," someone says in *The Confidence-Man,* which ultimately provides no firm philosophical place to stand, setting characters teetering between heart-hardening cynicism and foolish faith.

Confidence games, as well as magic shows and other forms of trickery, point to a human desire to be deceived, openness to illusion and enjoyment of misdirection. According to P. T. Barnum, "the public appears disposed to be amused even when they are conscious of being deceived." Admiration for con artists endures, as the countless Hollywood movies about them shows. (David Mamet's *House of Games* is a personal favorite.) "The grand points of human nature are the same

- 56 -

today they were a thousand years ago," Melville writes in *The Confidence-Man*. "The only variability in them is in expression, not in feature." The worrisome implications of this eager willingness to believe caused Melville to consider religious faith using different approaches in different novels.

Melville favors the skeptics over the worshippers, the doubters over the devout, the questioners over those who think they have all the answers. Pondering the pursuit of knowledge in the earlier, more famous novel *Moby-Dick* (1851), Melville's narrator Ishmael distinguishes between fast and loose fish and suggests that meaning is a loose-fish. Ishmael is troubled by the meaninglessness of the universe as he perceives it, but is also unwilling to stop studying it. He continues speculating and reconsidering. He does this knowing he will never catch any ultimate meaning. (I think of Ishmael as a fictional precursor to Albert Camus, who, nearly a century later, wrote: "I continue to believe that this world has no ultimate meaning. But I know that something in it has a meaning and that is man, because he is the only creature to insist on having one.") Presuming, like Ahab does, that the literal and metaphorical fish he pursues can be made fast produces tragic results. The captain will not abandon his vengeful, ultimately fatal, search for Moby Dick, but Ishmael accepts that some fish simply cannot be made fast, that some questions cannot be answered, that answers only lead to more questions. Ishmael's digressive narrative amounts to a massive refutation of Ahab's single-mindedness, his unshakeable conviction in what he's chosen to believe.

Ishmael overtly mocks and derides religions throughout *Moby-Dick*. The narrator says he cherishes "the greatest respect toward everybody's religious obligations, never mind how comical." There are limits to his respect, however:

> Now ... I have no objection to any person's religion, be it what it may, so long as that person does not kill or insult any other person, because that other person don't believe it also. But when a man's religion

becomes really frantic; when it is a positive torment to him; and, in fine, makes this earth of ours an uncomfortable inn to lodge in; then I think it high time to take that individual aside and argue the point with him.

Ishmael questions the relevance of religion to daily life; he observes that "a man's religion is one thing, and this practical world another." He also suspects that it's fundamentally wrong: "Methinks we have hugely mistaken this matter of Life and Death. Methinks that what they call my shadow here on earth is my true substance." He remarks on Christian hypocrisy: "Better to sleep with a sober cannibal than a drunken Christian"; "Christian kindness has proved but hollow courtesy." He says "Hell is an idea first born on an undigested apple-dumpling...."

In *The Confidence-Man*, Melville, adopting a philosopher-as-trickster mode, makes less overt but no less penetrating critiques of religious faith and the viability of Christianity. He challenges faith via sneaky dialogues in which Bible-quoting proponents of charity, confidence and trust are confidence men who reveal, to the reader, the pitfalls of the very virtues he purports to espouse. One of them describes the challenge of adhering to truth while remaining tolerant of those who do not:

[W]hen one is confident he has truth on his side, and that it is not on the other, it is no very easy thing to be charitable; not that temper is the bar, but conscience; for charity would beget toleration, you know, which is a kind of implied permitting, and in effect a kind of countenancing; and that which is countenanced is so far furthered. But should untruth be furthered?

After pointing out this conflict between Christian faith and charity, this person proceeds to convince an initially dismissive sick man, hoping to avoid "the appearance of a kind of implied irreligion," to extend his trust. As it happens, the persuader is an "herb-doctor" who sells the man his Omni-

Balsamic Reinvigorator, which requires the taker's confidence to work ("thriving not by the credulity of the simple, but the trust of the wise"). This healer doesn't want his new client to have confidence in his counterparts selling similar wares, of course, but only in him. After making the sale, he warns against counterfeits. Delbanco cites another passage describing misanthropy as a lack of confidence in kindness that, for all its "right and wise" praise of love, is similarly spoken by a con-man trying to win a doubter's trust.

FIFTH INTERLUDE

In Cannibals and Christians *(1966), Norman Mailer distinguishes between two types of essay collections: those that belong to their subjects and those that belong to their author. All the pieces bundled here concern holidays and closely related ideas and phenomena. Yet, at the risk of Mailerian immodesty, I aim for the kind of collection that encompasses a vision of existence and finds meaning in the relationships between disparate things. This is why, in contemplating my purported subject, I write about my own experience.*

Setting matters. I've lived in several different places. If Detroit, where I lived for more than twenty years and where I returned after a fifteen-year absence, shaped my outlook, so did New York, where I resided for eleven years and to which I now turn.

PARTITIONS ON PARADE

For several years – in 2005, 2006, 2007 and 2009 – boxer Miguel Cotto's promoter arranged for him to fight at Madison Square Garden on the June night preceding the annual Puerto Rican Day Parade. (In 2010, Cotto and Company used Yankee Stadium instead.) Cotto has served as Grand Marshal in the event following a victory. His representation, an outfit called Top Rank, banked on the proven idea that allegiances based on the fighter's Puerto Rican background would sell tickets. Bob Arum, who heads Top Rank, generally is not as active in New York City as other major boxing promoters such as Don King and Cedric Kushner. His company organizes fights for numerous Spanish-speaking fighters and eagerly seeks to attract loyal Mexican and Puerto Rican fight fans by trumpeting the boxers' origins and backgrounds. His usual stomping grounds are in Las Vegas, but he regularly scheduled an event at the Garden on the weekend of the parade.

There is nothing at all unusual about what Arum and Cotto did on those summer nights in New York. (Arum once made a statement that has become representative of boxing business ethics. When a journalist pointed out contradictory statements the promoter had made, Arum explained: "Yesterday I was lying, today I am telling the truth.") Fighters have long been put, willingly or not, in the position of embodying concepts of race, ethnicity and nationality. Perhaps one of the most famous incidences of this occurred with the two fights between Joe Louis and Max Schmeling in the 1930s, in which Louis's identity as both a black man and an American took on special significance in bouts with a fighter seen, correctly or incorrectly, as an avatar of Nazi ideology. Don King proudly presents pugilists' pigmentation as being of pri-

- 61 -

mary interest in his promotions, especially if he is positing a black fighter against a white one. Selecting St. Patrick's Day as a time to stage a match between Irish boxers and opponents from elsewhere takes little imagination. The Garden hosted a 2006 bout pairing John Duddy and Luis "Yory Boy" Campas dubbed "Shamrocks & Sombreros," for example. During a stretch of the same year, all the claimants to the various sanctioning bodies' heavyweight championship belts hailed from republics of the former Soviet Union, and promoters seemed to long for the tense days of the Cold War in their efforts to drum up interest in their fights with U.S. boxers. One event was pitched as "America's Last Line of Defense." If only there had still been a Red Menace to fear (and the boxer from Kazakhstan had not been a U.S. citizen).

There is also nothing out of the ordinary, at least in New York City, in having a day devoted to a particular group. The Puerto Rican Day Parade is a massive event with thousands of attendees and participants, but there are other days and parades connected with other identities. Columbus Day in October is *de facto* Italian American Day, just as St. Patrick's Day is regarded as Irish American Day. Other squares on the calendar are reserved for other groups. Large Gay Pride parades are held on different summer days in different boroughs of the city.

For the most part, this identity-based scheduling generates little controversy. Brouhahas can occur when overlapping elements of identity – such as religion, sexuality and nationality – come into conflict, or, rather, their self-proclaimed representatives do. For instance, on St. Patrick's Day, New Yorkers argue about the compatibility of homosexuality and parading while wearing green. The religious beliefs of some celebrants inevitably come into play. Every year, organizers of the annual parade bar explicitly gay groups from participating in the march along Fifth Avenue, while such groups regularly seek to be allowed to join in the event. Obviously, not all individual homosexuals are excluded. All Catholic priests are automatically permitted to march, for example. However, those who believe that for conception to be immaculate there must be no sex involved (and that such a thing is possible) are famously queasy about the sort of people who engage in sexual activity that has no chance of resulting in pregnancy. They're simultaneously uncomfortable with sex and obsessed with what people are doing with their genitals. Even though the day clearly has a religious flavor – it's named for a saint, for Christ's sake – many regard it as primarily an occasion associated not with a specific creed but with a particular nationality, though one need not actually have ever been to Ireland, or even have an ancestor from the island, in order to celebrate. You don't have to engage in the ritual debate over homosexuality as long as you are on the sanctioned side of the question (or silent about it) and display a fondness for Kelly green. For the most part, however, events organized around narrowly defined ideas of identity have become routine matters.

If holidays should be communal events, as Barbara Ehrenreich, the author of *Dancing in the Streets: A History of Collective Joy* (2007), asserts, then days like these envision community in a manner that's as much about exclusion as inclusion. Community, here, is not just all the people living in the same location. These holidays posit differences and set a portion of the population apart from the rest. They apply identity politics to the calendar, staking claims to this day for this ethnic group, to that one for that nationality, and to another for a particular sexual preference. Instead of having a large and varied but still unified community, then, there are lots of smaller conclaves distinguished by their not being wholly a part of the larger populace.

Perhaps as a person who, if he were inclined to do such a thing, could trace his ancestry back to various European nations, I do not see the appeal, or know the joy, of privileging minority group status as the principal basis of self-conception. I can comprehend theoretically the desire to feel pride and strive for dignity in the face of humiliating treatment, but, not having suffered discrimination the way many others have, I've never felt a deep need to transform what bigots have devalued into something of great personal import. Choices I've made, interests I've developed, places I've lived, people I've known, enthusiasms I've nurtured – these are things I take to make up who I am. Things over which I've never had any control – the color of my skin, the birthplace of my great great grandparents – seem like accidental characteristics of no special significance.

When one hasn't had to struggle over issues of inherited identity, such things just don't seem to signify all that much. I've been told that I have some Irish blood on my mother's side, but St. Patrick's Day means nothing to me other than being a day that I want to avoid certain parts of Midtown Manhattan because of parade-related inconveniences. Some choose to make the annual march more of a challenge by impairing their ability to stand, let alone move forward in a straight line. Once, when I was new to the city, I found myself sharing the sidewalk with a man who was urinating as he walked along Fifth Avenue at lunchtime. Anyone who has been in the area on the holiday knows that this is not some discriminatory cliché about Irish drunkenness. Many of those revelers pursuing Ehrenreich's idea of collective joy on this day, whatever their background, simply opt to imbibe large quantities of beer and whiskey. It's tradition, after all. Polish heritage on my father's side never made me want to root for Andrew "Foul Pole" Golota when I attended fights involving the Polish boxer infamous for throwing low blows. My purported claims to a Lithuanian background never made me more (or less) inclined to cheer for fighters who came from behind the Iron Curtain.

I have attended enough boxing matches to know that many others do not look at these things the way I do. Indeed, the assumption of partiality and national solidarity is built into the process of judging bouts in a manner that reinforces such subjectivity instead of encouraging neutrality. A fight at the Garden between, say, a prominent Puerto Rican like Cotto and a Mexican opponent is likely to have a judge from Puerto Rico on one side of the ring, a judge from Mexico on another, with the last judge from a third country. Rather than selecting three disinterested judges, regardless of their background, organizers of boxing matches assume allegiances are at play and that the third supposedly objective judge will counterbalance the other two. Any contest decided by judges' votes, whether it's a beauty pageant, or the Academy Awards, or a fight with a victory not determined by knockout, is necessarily imperfect, its outcome open to debate. Boxing is especially notorious for bad decisions, such as Roy Jones, Jr.'s loss in the 1988 Seoul Olympics to Korean fighter Park Si-Hun, who apologized to Jones afterward for the judges' injudicious ruling. This is also the case with small-scale events not including combatants from different countries. "Hometown decisions" are ones where the local fighter seems favored in close, or not so close, contests with fighters from other places. (When Cotto fought in New York in June, he enjoyed the position of the hometown fighter, even when he faced opponents from the city, such as Yuri Foreman in 2010, Zab Judah in 2007 and Paul Malignaggi in 2006.) The prejudices presumed to be influencing judges clearly affect what many vocal fight fans see, or choose to see. The person yelling the loudest is often the least informed, but knowledge of boxing and the ability to assess which fighter is more skillful, more effective, more aggressive and better able to defend himself doesn't matter if all a specific athlete's supporters really care about is his racial, religious, ethnic or national identity.

Identity as an American does not depend on blood or soil. U.S. citizens can have been born anywhere and be of any color. They don't even need to share the ideas of liberty on which the nation was founded, though the freedom to make choices about what to think and where to go – the sort of freedom of self-creation I've enjoyed – is surely part of the country's appeal to immigrants who continue to make it their home. I do not want to suggest that celebrants of holidays devoted to a less broad notion of identity are doing something contradictory to the spirit of the American ideal. Clearly, they are not. However, I think the idea of communal celebrations – indeed, the idea of a country – where race, color and ancestry are irrelevancies rather than priorities is something to strive for.

It may be crucial to reconsider the way we think about these things, since giving special emphasis to a particular identity can have consequences far graver than biased assessment of a boxer's performance. Amartya Sen, in his 2006 book *Identity and Violence: The Illusion of Destiny*, describes the way that ignoring the multiple "affiliations, priorities, and pursuits" that a person has both diminishes individuals and contributes to the world's already considerable turmoil. He expresses concern about religious identity being made a person's exclusive identity (but the move can be seen being made in other areas as well). "The increasing tendency to overlook the many identities that any human being has and to try to classify individuals according to a single allegedly pre-eminent religious identity is an intellectual confusion that can animate dangerous divisiveness," he writes. Sen is particularly troubled by the willingness of both "Islamist instigator[s] of violence" and "those who would like to quell that violence" to insist on such reductive thinking. "The world is made much more incendiary by the advocacy and popularity of single-dimension categorizations of human beings, which combine haziness of vision with increased scope for the exploitation of that haze by the champions of violence."

I am not equating holiday parade routes with the paths taken by murderous religious fundamentalists. That would be simplistic. Besides, the focus on an elastic definition of ethnic heritage (being "green" if only for one day) might dilute the religious content of St. Patrick's Day. However, what Sen calls "incarcerating people within the enclosures of a single identity" can be seen in connection with travelers on both types of road. Insisting on "a choiceless singularity of human identity" constricts reason and volition, according to Sen. Results of this impulse can be as severe as catastrophic violence against "infidels"; divisive, demagogic politics involving appeals to spurious "celebrations" of "diversity"; or the relatively trivial misjudgment of the regulated violence confined to the boxing ring. But no matter where the outcomes fall along the spectrum of seriousness, I'm uncomfortable with classifying people in a way that venerates such all-encompassing singular identities, whether in terms of nationality or religion or sexuality or race or language or status – even if it is just for a particular day of the year.

Obviously, only in an ahistorical fantasyland could anyone suggest that such "partitions" (as Sen calls them) were not factors, even the primary factors, in how U.S. residents came to think of themselves, whether through their own choices or the impositions of others. The ideal of freedom to which I referred above remains an ideal not fully realized. But that does not mean its realization shouldn't remain a goal.

I suspect that defining what we are on the basis of what we are not, which is what reinforcing partitions does, works against such an aim. Yet I doubt this is even a consideration for identity-focused celebrants. Evidently, there are always people some will designate as outsiders, even if they live in the same place. Some even find this sort of thing fun. That doesn't strike me as something to celebrate.

SIXTH INTERLUDE

One of the most frequent, and least interesting, questions flung at nonbelievers asks how we explain the origins of the universe and everything in it without crediting some divine master builder. I don't pretend to have all the answers. Nor can I pretend that imagining or inheriting fantastic scenarios that purport to solve all mysteries actually does. Whenever someone says, of whatever all-encompassing system of belief he or she fancies, "it's the only thing that makes sense," you can be confident that you're hearing nonsense. None of us knows everything.

There will always be things we don't understand – and for me baseball is one of them …

OPENING DAY SHUTOUT

In an uncustomary relaxation of the stern and rigid discipline that defined it, the parochial school I attended from seventh to twelfth grades permitted students whose parents obtained tickets for opening day to look at live baseball instead of dull blackboards. I can't recall if this happened every year. Maybe the Detroit club's World Series victory in 1984 spurred a single spell of civic enthusiasm the following season. I do know that at least one afternoon toward the end of a school year I took advantage of this free pass from class and went with my father to the since-razed ballpark at the corner of Michigan Avenue and Trumbull Street.

Now before anyone starts to expect a moist-eyed, sentimental look back at a long-distant day when skies were bluer and grass was greener and fathers and sons bonded over the all-American game of baseball in that innocent era before players' performances were artificially enhanced, I want to make something absolutely clear: that opening day wasn't the start of a lifelong love of baseball. That's just not my story. I don't like that damn game and never have. I can't say I hate baseball because I've never felt so strongly about it. I did play little league ball for a few seasons before I found better things to do, but even then I didn't want to watch the game. The standing around with nothing to do that tried the patience of many a ten-year-old outfielder was at least punctuated by the occasional need to chase a ball. Players do get to bat periodically. But for me the long stretches of inactivity that inhibited enjoyment of playing ruled out becoming a spectator. At least in sports like basketball and football all the participants are usually active *at the same time*. Watching someone swing a stick while others loiter on manicured lawns is not my idea of a good time. I have no use for golf either. A television sports commentator once told me that in all sports players try to impose their wills via intermediaries like balls and pucks. The more direct the imposition, the more viscerally exciting the sport will be. The convolutions involved in baseball players' rather indirect self assertions might make their endeavor complex, and perhaps this theory explains the game's appeal to intellectual types, but I don't think it really accounts for eagerness to watch baseball as opposed to, say, chess or croquet.

Here I should make one more thing perfectly plain: I don't categorically dismiss sports or those who follow them. Indifference to baseball may indelibly mark an American male as a misfit, but this one is not insensible to the various reasons for fascination with athletics. I'm not one of those people who thinks aggressive competitiveness ought to be discouraged or that watching others engaged in it is necessarily a waste of time. I know that great athletes excel not only because of luck in the genetic lottery but also because of countless hours of training. The discipline, tenacity, focus, hard work and commitment required to succeed deserve widespread admiration. Athletes can display grace, poise and mental as well as physical strength – a potent combination of valuable qualities. Seeing fit people performing difficult maneuvers well can be an aesthetic experience. I can entertain the notion that to examine the propensity to play and watch games is to explore what it means to be human. In the abstract, I see how all of this applies to baseball, but since it applies equally to other sports, none of it explains the pervasive appeal of that game in particular.

Because baseball matters so much to so many people in the United States, I've wondered if it didn't offer a route to comprehending the national character. Film director Ken Burns took that idea as the premise for his eighteen-and-half-hour 1994 documentary *Baseball* and its four-hour 2010 follow-up *Baseball: The Tenth Inning*. He told *The New York Times* that "baseball is a way to understand American history" and I suspect that there's enough sense in that idea to take it seriously. For some groups, embracing baseball meant assimilating into American society. Jackie Robinson's breaking through the wall that barred black players from major league baseball, to cite but one example, is no simple sports story. Burns revisited the sport he'd already scrutinized at length because of developments like the 1994 players' strike and the scandal of rampant steroid use.

Yet almost any sport can reveal something about a society. Take one I do understand. "The history of boxing is the mirror image of America's immigrant experience," journalist Jack Newfield contends. "Every immigrant group, living in slums, seeking an American identity, had fighters as their first heroes." Newfield's friend Budd Schulberg, who authored stories such as "Meal Ticket" illustrating precisely this point, also developed a theory about the heavyweight championship, namely "that somehow each of the great figures to hold the title manages to sum up the spirit of his time." (With twentieth-century titans on his mind, Schulberg was writing at a time when boxing had much cultural cachet and boxers could still be described as "great figures.") Thirty-nine years before Robinson donned a Brooklyn Dodgers uniform in 1947, Jack Johnson defiantly broke down a barrier by becoming the first black heavyweight champion. Robinson was named the National League's most valuable player in 1949, the same year Joe Louis's twelve-year reign as champion ended, and the baseball player credited the widely esteemed boxer's accomplishments for making his possible. Certainly, the transformation of Cassius Clay into Muhammad Ali, who espoused a separatist ideology even while working with white associates and belittling black opponents, is an odyssey that illustrates something crucial about race in America, even if the meaning remains ambiguous. Although unorganized fighters couldn't bring about the work-stoppage equivalent of the cancellation of the 1994 World Series, the exploitation of most boxers, the massive purses won by a few and the enrichment of controversial characters like ex-convict and promoter Don King surely exposes much about the U.S. economic system. And juiced batters are hardly the only people seeking unfair advantages. In his effort to understand his country, Burns could have looked at a sport other than baseball (and he did when he made *Unforgivable Blackness,* a rather lengthy documentary about Johnson).

Still, something about baseball sets it apart. I've read of an effort to make opening day a national holiday. Even if this drive were only partially in earnest, enough adults do take time away from work to fill stadiums on the first day game of a season. That a school more eager to recognize religious than secular holidays and not usually lax about attendance would conclude that going to a game could take precedence over studying also suggests that people really do think baseball fundamentally matters.

Left indifferent (bored, actually) by that long ago home opener and a few other trips to ballparks over the years, and unable to imagine sacrificing a day of my life to sitting through Burns's baseball movies (fine films though they may be), I had to look elsewhere in my attempt to solve the mystery of the sport. Where better to turn than literature in a quest to understand human endeavors? Schulberg, author of several fictional and nonfictional books concerning boxing, allows that only baseball rivals his and my preferred sport in the quantity and quality of literature it has inspired. Certainly I've read some incisive stories in which baseball plays a big part, but with the best of these (like David James Duncan's *The Brothers K*), I've enjoyed them *despite* the sport's presence. This might not seem like praise, but it is. By force of individual voice and style, the most able writers can hold the attention even of readers usually uninterested in their subject matter, or so I believe. Besides, contests inherently involve drama – the ecstasy of winning and the agony of losing, the David-and-Goliath scenario, the conflict between cowboys in black hats and white hats, and so on – and sports offer settings where intense emotions can play themselves out in all their glory and shame. The specific organized conflict matters less than the desire and disappointment generated. If these are realized fully and depicted vividly, then it doesn't matter if the tale revolves around baseball, beach volleyball or a spelling bee. But writers' enthrallment with certain games may not be contagious, especially when they concentrate intently on the particulars and minutiae of a sport (especially when it's baseball). I've read stories that might please fans but moved me to look elsewhere for amusement (much as baseball games on television do). No matter how I try to enter these stories, baseball bars the door.

Don DeLillo received much acclaim for the opening portion of *Underworld,* which involves the homerun that dramatically ended a storied 1951 game sequence, but I think he might have gotten close to something essential and unsettling about the sport and its adherents at the start of another novel. DeLillo begins *Mao II* with a huge Moonie wedding at Yankee Stadium, where one of the thirteen thousand participants simultaneously marrying strangers designated by their Master thinks about two words. Of "baseball," Karen Janney muses: "The word has resonance if you're American, a sense of shared heart and untranslatable lore." The other word she contemplates, as her father worries that she's surrendering her "singularities" as she merges with the "undifferentiated mass" on the field, is "cult." Perhaps fandom too involves true believer's abandonment of individuality, submission to an external power and the performance of rituals. "They stand and chant," DeLillo writes, "fortified by the blood of numbers." He could be referring to the Moonies, but he could be commenting on those cheering followers of that field's usual occupants. Like the couples in *Mao II* who wed partners chosen by their charismatic leader, baseball fans swear allegiance to players selected by teams' calculating owners. Those performing the rites of fanaticism through one endless baseball season after another certainly display comparable devotion to organizations they don't control and commitment to lore that cannot be translated to outsiders.

Sporting events and religious ceremonies have even more in common than the sense of belonging to a community and related non-rational loyalties. In addition to the chanting DeLillo mentions, there's often music, sometimes with call- and-response moments, in both arenas and churches. There are prayer-like moments of silence for deceased group members (whether fellow congregants or former players). There are "miracles" that appear to defy logical explanations of how the physical world works (Jesus walking on water, James "Buster" Douglas knocking out Mike Tyson). Ardent devotees of sports and religion certainly share the desire to accumulate esoteric information (arcane texts, batting averages).

If imputing a religious air to baseball dedication overstates its depth, doing so at least imputes a degree of seriousness to what otherwise looks like an astonishing amount of time spent serially watching inconsequential diversions. DeLillo, I know, didn't mean to disparage baseball in *Mao II*. He's another novelist enamored by the game. Baseball, he told *The Observer*, "was just so natural, because we all grew up with it. We played it; we listened to it on the radio, and then we went to Yankee Stadium. It was a taken-for-granted pleasure." Far from vaguely sinister worshipfulness, it's just something fun. This, of course, assumes one does take pleasure in the game – in listening to it, in watching it, in talking about it. I will say this much for all sports, including baseball: the athletes do exist and what they do can be observed, which makes it both different from and superior to religions, with their nonexistent beings that are said to do so much.

Several other writers I enviously admire share my lack of enthusiasm for baseball. They have nothing to do with my attitude, since it formed before I ever read them. I admit, however, that knowing they viewed this topic as I do gave me an extra reason to like them. (Similarly, learning that John Coltrane had to ask, "Who's Willie Mays, Jim?" when a fellow musician began talking about a recent game boosted my fondness for him even though his ingenuous baseball obliviousness in no way affects the sound of his saxophone.) In *The Sweet Science,* essayist A.J. Liebling remarks that he "never cared much about baseball," even though he did attend some Yankee games when he was young. (Along the same lines, Schulberg recalls a youthful fascination with lightweight Benny Leonard so complete it left him unable to care about legends like Babe Ruth and Ty Cobb breaking silly batting records.) In *A Neutral Corner,* Liebling says that when Yankee Stadium was made the staging area for a 1959 fight it was "converted ... to a noble purpose" – as distinct from its usual, something-other-than-noble one. Twenty years earlier, in 1939, Louis had fought the first heavyweight championship bout ever held in Detroit when he defended his title against Bob Pastor at what was then known as Briggs Stadium. I might have thought of that piece of trivia in conjunction with Liebling's line had I known either when I was sitting four and half decades later in what by then had been renamed Tiger Stadium. I certainly wanted something to ponder other than what I saw before me.

George Orwell objected to sports because of the ugliness they brought out in people when games cease to be about fun and fitness and start to shoulder symbolism: "as soon as the question of prestige arises, as soon as you feel that you and some larger unit will be disgraced if you lose, the most savage combative instincts are aroused." Orwell worries especially about athletes becoming national representatives. "At the international level sport is frankly mimic warfare," Orwell writes in "The Sporting Spirit," a 1945 *Tribune* column. "But the significant thing is not the behaviour of the players but the attitude of the spectators: and, behind the spectators, of the nations who work themselves into furies over these absurd contests, and seriously believe – at any rate for short periods – that running, jumping and kicking a ball are tests of national virtue." Orwell frets about football (or what Americans call soccer), cricket and the Olympics inflaming vicious patriotic passions; he dislikes boxing because "a fight between white and coloured boxers before a mixed audience" can fuel racial hatred. Since he was writing during Louis's era, Orwell might have been thinking of the two fights with Max Schmeling, a boxer regarded both inside and outside his native Germany as the poster boy of the Nazis' racist fantasies.

Orwell misses something crucial here. I've been at fights where it was immediately evident that the loudest spectators didn't know what they were shouting about when it came to boxing itself and based their preferences on criteria other than athletic ability. But even if countless vocal partisans root for whom they root because of racism or nationalism, this doesn't mean the game is to blame. Besides, even if mixed race contests antagonized imbeciles, by taking part in such events athletes like Jack Johnson, Joe Louis and Jackie Robinson became heroes, at least to some, and contributed, at least to some degree, to positive change in racial attitudes. Orwell is right that athletes have at times been burdened with out-of-proportion symbolism and that the worst kinds of bloody-minded ignorance can be heard in sporting arenas, but his dislike for the ugliness blinds him to the glimpses of beauty sports can offer.

Gay Talese looked like a better candidate for cracking the enigma of baseball. After all, he has none of the usually dependable Orwell's reflexive aversion to sports. Talese wrote numerous essays on boxing as well as baseball. Someone who finds fighters intriguing and can convey something meaningful about them should be able to articulate the grounds for baseball adoration. Or so I reasoned when I picked up *The Silent Season of a Hero: The Sports Writing of Gay Talese.*

As it turns out, the collection leaves the impression that Talese doesn't care much for sports at all. The sports matter only insofar as his subjects' reactions to contests reveal something about their characters. He writes about individuals, really. Sports figures, especially those whose best days are behind them, often have compelling stories, and these interest Talese even if the ones he tells have little or nothing to do with the games that gave his subjects their fame. (Golf comes up with disheartening frequency in his profiles of former fighters and baseball players.) The title essay looks at Joe DiMaggio fifteen years after he retired from baseball and twenty five years after "he hit in fifty-six straight games and became the most cherished man in America." Talese shadows DiMaggio as he avoids talking about former wife Marilyn Monroe, attends to business obligations, chats with fans who recall his glory days and plays golf. His profile of Joe Louis at age forty-eight uses exactly the same formula, describing the former champion's post-boxing business, his interactions with admirers, his love of golf. The only real difference is that Louis doesn't mind talking about his ex-wives. Talese penned numerous pieces on boxer Floyd Patterson (thirty-seven of them, according to editor Michael Rosenwald). Those reprinted in *The Silent Season* look at what Patterson did when he wasn't in the ring, like routinely carrying a fake beard so he could sneak away from an arena unrecognized if were to lose a fight, which reveals something about a man's insecurities but nothing about his sport.

Talese's vignettes often have little to do with sports in any essential way. The pieces on DiMaggio and Louis could have been about pop singers, actors, politicians or others whose profession previously, briefly made them renowned. When investigating the exceptional well after their prime, Talese shows more interest in their long treks downward than in their earlier ascents and the peaks they'd reached. No one would care about Louis's golf obsession if he hadn't been an astounding fighter, but Talese doesn't bother recounting his ring exploits. Talese takes it as a given that DiMaggio was once a beloved hero without troubling himself to explain why repeatedly hitting small balls made him one. Talese's approach might yield better literature than more conventional reportage on a game or a fight ever could. No knowledge of or even interest in the sports he purportedly covers is required. But if someone truly does want to learn something about the sports themselves, then he or she must turn elsewhere.

I had hoped Stephen Jay Gould's *The Richness of Life* would give me insight into baseball as well as evolution. I knew of Gould's enthusiasm for the subjects and that the collection addressed both of them; I thought that someone who could clearly explain complicated scientific theories to a non-specialist audience might also articulate the cause of the sport's appeal. He explains DiMaggio's famous hitting streak in a way that conveys its significance – its extreme improbability – but hardly made me want to sit through hour after hour of baseball just in case something equally rare might occur.

I wouldn't have gone on the opening day outing if I'd known that baseball is just math class by other means. (Perhaps my old school knew what they were doing after all.) Gould elucidates the statistical anomalies expressed by accomplishments like DiMaggio's, but I have no desire to sit in the stands computing. He can also explain plate tectonics. I think continents drift at a faster rate than the average baseball game moves, but this doesn't make me want to watch shifting land masses either.

Game guides like Gould point out that even the best players fail to hit the ball much more frequently than they connect. And yet I gather that, despite batters' strong tendency to miss, a pitcher throwing a no-hitter represents baseball at its best. As far as I can tell, this amounts to a game of catch between the pitcher and the fellow crouching behind home plate, with perhaps, occasionally, a few fouls and other failures.

Failure – now that's something I can understand. As in failure to figure out what millions of other natural born citizens grasp intuitively and transplants pick up with alacrity. As in failure to feel the resonance of the word *baseball*. (In that already quoted *Observer* interview, DeLillo calls baseball his "second language." It's one I failed to learn.) As in failure to muster even a modicum of interest in the World Series, if I even notice when it takes place. As in failure, until absurdly late in life, to perceive the wisdom of John Coltrane, who tuned out what didn't matter to him in order to focus raptly on what did.

SEVENTH INTERLUDE

It's possible to draw up a list of objections to the Ten Commandments longer than the Decalogue itself. Chief among the reasons for disapproval would be the fact that, as so often happens with the Bible, there are multiple discrepant versions of the laws in different chapters of different books (namely Exodus and Deuteronomy). Even if we stick with just one compendium of the rules for upright living passed along by Moses, there remains the faulty premise that humans require such divine direction and the related implication that they wouldn't or couldn't devise and respect, say, prohibitions against stealing that didn't have heavenly authority backing them up. As Julian the Apostate observed, the reason within us can provide a pretty good guide to what we ought to do and what we ought to refrain from doing.

Beyond the fundamental but general causes for disesteem there are particular problems with several of the enjoinders. Some – the first four, for instance – call for satisfying the demands of a rather needy despot rather than provide guidance for moral behavior. People can quite easily not recognize the speaker in the first commandment as their lord and disregard the subsequent injunctions regarding carved images, names taken in vain and Sabbath day observations and still act decently toward one another. (The indicated punishment for breaking these rules, by the way, is often death, which the list's vocal champions usually don't mention, an omission that – I hope – indicates they don't really know the Bible as well as they pretend.) The tenth, which prohibits coveting this and that, concerns what people think or desire rather than what they actually do – a worrisomely totalitarian legislative precedent.

Others call for nice enough gestures and deeds but under-

- 80 -

mine them precisely by making them compulsory. Following rules because one fears punishment surely stands as a lower order of ethics than freely choosing to do the right thing simply because it is the right thing. Similarly, honoring people because you are ordered to do so degrades and diminishes the insisted upon act. One can only truly honor another by voluntarily doing so. What bothers me about the central part of the fifth commandment – Honor thy father and thy mother – is the presumption that I need to be told to do so.

WHOLLY HONORABLE

Other than the possibly unintentional echo of the fifth of the Ten Commandments, there is nothing essentially religious about Mother's Day or Father's Day. Of course, that doesn't mean the faithful refrained from bringing religion into their observation. Yet on the second Sunday in May and the third Sunday in June, two wholly honorable and honorably non-holy days, any such faithful fare can be disregarded.

Although days devoted to motherhood with supernatural inflections (such as links to various goddesses like Cybele in ancient Greece) preceded it, the Mother's Day initiated in the United States in the early twentieth century aimed to honor mothers, plain and simple. Ann Jarvis dreamed of a holiday to reunite families sundered by the Civil War but died before the idea caught on. Her daughter, Anna Jarvis, chose to remember her mother by making Mother's Day an actual national holiday. With her participation, the first celebration was held in 1908, and President Woodrow Wilson made it official six years later. After learning of Jarvis's effort, Sonora Smart Dodd decided male parents deserved equivalent recognition and initiated a campaign for Father's Day, which didn't receive the presidential imprimatur until Richard Nixon signed a law making it a national holiday in 1972. Although rival claimants for thinking up these complementary celebrations do (or did) exist, Jarvis and Dodd typically receive the credit.

In any case, what's important is that the days were designed to encourage people to appreciate their parents, which can be done in completely secular fashion. Whatever the grounds I have for refusing to celebrate Easter, Christmas and some other holidays, I see no earthly reason to ignore these two (unless particular, horrible parents deserve no tribute, that is). Soon before Mother's Day in 2013, novelist Anne Lamott wrote an article called "Why I Hate Mother's Day" for *Salon* in which she contends that the day "perpetuates the dangerous idea that *all* parents are somehow superior to non-parents." This is nonsense stumbling about on stilts. I assume Lamott would say the same charge applies to the day's masculine counterpart, but, as a childless man, I can say that Father's Day never made me feel inferior to those who reproduced. Presidents' Day never made me feel less worthy than those elected to the nation's highest office either. Mother's Day does not exist to insult non-parents, and until I read Lamott's silly screed I'd never encountered anyone confused enough to think that it did.

When on a certain spring day I told my mother that after a decade and a half of living in distant cities I was moving back home to Detroit, she said it was the best Mother's Day gift I could've given her. I take great satisfaction in that, especially since I know my disinclination to follow other holidays' conventions at times annoyed her. It's good to know my proximity meant more to her than a carnation or a piece of jewelry, two more conventional gifts.

For plenty of people churchgoing routinely figures into Mother's Day, preachers make use of readymade material for sermons, and Catholics often associate it with the Virgin Mary, but these religious components are strictly optional. Leaving them out doesn't violate the spirit of the holiday the way attempts to edit out the scriptural or spiritual parts of truly god-centric holidays does. (People do skip them when it comes to honoring male parents. A survey of pastors conducted in 2012 by a Christian research firm called LifeWay found that Mother's Day trailed only Easter and Christmas in church attendance, but Father's Day didn't get people into pews.) With untroubled minds and no compromise of their principles, humanists may honor their parents on these designated days (and others) despite the superfluous biblical insistence that they do so.

EIGHTH INTERLUDE

Turning one's back on long-lived traditions can make one appear dour or bereft of community spirit, but a humanist perspective allows ample space for celebration, I believe. I may (somewhat hyperbolically) call holidays disasters, but fairness and accuracy, as well as respect for worthwhile traditions, require that I acknowledge a holiday commemorating the end of a disaster.

Juneteenth has been called the oldest celebration marking the end of slavery in the United States (although Emancipation Day, celebrated in former British colonies in the Caribbean and parts of the United States is a rival for that distinction). It was on June 19, 1865 – two and a half years after the Emancipation Proclamation formally went into effect and one day after Union troops arrived in Galveston to actually implement it – that General Gordon Granger declared: "The people of Texas are informed that, in accordance with a proclamation from the Executive of the United States, all slaves are free."

Now that is worth celebrating. There were a quarter of a million slaves in Texas at the end of the Civil War. The freed men and women or (more likely) their descendants who during the following century joined the Great Migration to northern and western states carried with them such Juneteenth traditions as public readings of Abraham Lincoln's shackle-shattering Proclamation, family reunions, cookouts lubricated with red soda pop and, yes, prayer services (and even baseball!).

Internal migrants in search of new beginnings also took different holiday habits with them, and added new meaning to others. Transplants from rural areas of the South continued to shoot their guns in the air on New Year's Eve, a less salutary practice that persisted well into the twenty-first century in places like Detroit. Whatever the merits or demerits of trying to recast Easter as a theologically neutral day of symbolic rebirth, its metaphorical possibilities for those embarking on quests for another, freer way of living are undeniable. (Of course, many of these travelers would have had no desire to deny them anyway.) Then again, as I point out in the following pages, migrants leaving the South and heading north on Easter had a very real practical aspect too. The Fourth of July – a more widely acknowledged day for the exultation of independence than Juneteenth – was another oft-selected time for heading north – or for returning to visit relatives who had stayed put.

THE OVERGROUND RAILROAD BLUES

Travelers file through congested doorways under signs announcing distant destinations: Chicago, New York, St. Louis. Crowds of men and women with all the belongings they can carry walk beneath a line of birds aloft in a flight of their own. A black train engine shines a bright light forward through the deep blue of the night sky. A slumped figure sits alone on a rock near a tree branch from which a dark noose dangles. Three black men stand linked by bulky shackles and look outside through thick prison bars. Three girls in red, yellow and blue dresses reach up to write numbers on a chalkboard. Black women, men and children crowd a train station platform. Such scenes make up *The Migration of the Negro* series, sixty thematically connected paintings for which artist Jacob Lawrence provided explanatory captions. Of those setting off on a journey in the first panel, he says: "During the World War there was a great migration North by Southern Negroes." Of those emulating birds, he says: "In every town Negroes were leaving by the hundreds to go North and enter into Northern industry." Stressing that economics alone could not explain the exodus, Lawrence says of the rope-draped limb: "Another cause was lynching. It was found that where there had been a lynching, the people who were reluctant to leave at first left immediately after this." About the men in jail, he comments: "Another of the social causes of the migrants' leaving was that at times they did not feel safe, or it was not the best thing to be found on the streets late at night. They were arrested on the slightest provocation."

There's still more that accounts for the phenomenon Lawrence depicts than jobs in states like Illinois, Michigan and New York and rampant injustice and violence in states like

Louisiana, Mississippi and Florida. With regards to those colorfully clad pupils, he notes: "In the North the Negro had better educational facilities." For a multitude of reasons, the people continued to move. "And the migrants kept coming," Lawrence says of those waiting for a train in the last picture in his series.

Indeed, they kept coming for another three decades after Lawrence completed *The Migration of the Negro* in 1941. What came to be known as the Great Migration did start with the First World War, during which more than half a million blacks left the South, a greater number than had decamped in the fifty years after Abraham Lincoln issued the Emancipation Proclamation. Prior to the war's outbreak, only a trickle of blacks seeped out of the South. By disrupting the supply of European immigrants to the Northern states, the conflict created openings for Southern black workers, who moved rapidly to fill them. Yet the end of the war did not dam the stream, which did not stop flowing until the 1960s ended. (During the 1960s, some of travelers included those on so-called Reverse Freedom Rides. White Citizens' Councils in the South, responding to integration efforts involving northerners like the Freedom Rides, bought one-way bus and train tickets for black people, who were often misled to believe jobs would be waiting for them. Some tickets were purchased to Hyannis, Massachusetts, near the Kennedy family compound, as an attempt to embarrass President John F. Kennedy, whom segregationists believed was an ardent supporter of the civil rights movement.) In a little more than half a century, approximately six million black southerners made their way to other parts of the country, transforming themselves and their new homes profoundly in the process. Only about ten percent of all black Americans lived outside the South in 1915, a half century after the end of the Civil War; almost half did by 1970, the endpoint of the Great Migration.

This was no mere reconfiguration of demographic patterns. The Great Migration altered the nation in fundamental ways, challenging the separate and unequal, racially delineated arrangements that characterized the South after Reconstruction and spurring the civil rights movement. Those who slipped the strictures of Jim Crow discovered what it was like not to have to step off sidewalks to let white pedestrians pass, not to have to use "colored" waiting rooms and bank teller windows, not to have to enter buildings by their back doors and ride only in freight elevators, not to have every aspect of their daily existence humiliatingly codified, and not to live with the knowledge that they could be hanged without trial or provocation. They could sit wherever they chose on buses and trains. They could vote.

Furthermore, they wrote of what they found and sent money to those who remained behind, many of whom subsequently followed, carrying bits of the South with them, like the tradition of eating black-eyed peas for good luck on New Year's Day. The depletion of the South's pool of cheap labor, coupled with the growing awareness among black Americans that a different, less confining way of living was possible, put pressure on the segregated South to change even before legislation like the Civil Rights Act of 1964 required it to do so. In *The Warmth of Other Suns* (2010), Isabel Wilkerson calls this "perhaps one of the biggest underreported stories of the twentieth century." And it's an unfinished story, as the reverse migration of black Americans from the North to the South in the early twenty-first century attests.

The Great Migration did not stem from anything so simple as economic opportunity, Wilkerson insists. It was messier than that, and gloriously so. "It wasn't one thing," she says of what motivated migrants. "It was everything." Of those who continued moving even after World War I ended she writes: "Theirs is a kind of living testimony that migrations fed by the human heart do not begin and end as neatly as statisticians might like." She doesn't skip facts and figures, but she cares most about the hopes and longings underlying them.

If Lawrence had already covered some of the same territory, Wilkerson endeavors to give a richer, fuller version of the event he chronicled at its midpoint. Besides looking at the entire time span, she looks at participants in a different way. In many paintings, Lawrence presents featureless, anonymous figures, virtual stand-ins for anyone of African descent. (Scholar Leslie King-Hammond discusses this aspect of Lawrence's work in an essay included in *Over the Line: The Art and Life of Jacob Lawrence,* edited by Peter T. Nesbett and Michelle DuBois and published in conjunction with an exhibition of the same name that toured several U.S. cities from 2001 to 2003.) Wilkerson, in contrast, eschews crowd scenes, preferring portraits. She animates *The Warmth of Other Suns* with three particular individuals' intimate stories: Ida Mae Brandon Gladney, who in the late 1930s left rural Mississippi for Milwaukee before settling in Chicago; George Swanson Starling, who in the mid-1940s fled central Florida for New York City; and Robert Joseph Pershing Foster, who in the 1950s left Monroe, Louisiana, for Los Angeles. Rather than making them functionally representative figures, Wilkerson intertwines detailed biographies of her protagonists, fleshed-out narratives of unique lives whose paths never crossed, to convey a sense of what it was like to be a part of a huge internal migration.

For all their individuality, these three people permit Wilkerson to trace some broad tendencies. Established transportation routes determined the three main routes migrants used. These bus and train lines formed "the Overground Railroad for slavery's grandchildren," writes Wilkerson. One track, which Ida Mae Gladney took, essentially ran alongside the Mississippi River from Alabama, Arkansas, Mississippi and Tennessee to industrial centers in Michigan, Illinois, Ohio, Pennsylvania and Wisconsin (which goes some way toward explaining why Chicago bluesmen with Delta lineage sang so many songs about locomotives). Another ferried people like George Starling from the Carolinas, Georgia, Florida and Virginia up the east coast to Washington, New York City and

Boston. A third trail, blazed later than the others, saw black Southerners from Louisiana and Texas head to California, as Robert Foster did, and to other points west.

These migrants had a great deal in common with others coming to the United States from foreign countries. With strictly pragmatic economic migration, roamers usually go as short a way as necessary to satisfy their need for income, but Wilkerson's migrants resembled "the vast movements of refugees from famine, war, and genocide in other parts of the world, where oppressed people ... go great distances." Robert Foster, she says, went to California because he "was going to be a citizen of the United States, like the passport said." Yet even symbolic actions can have a practical side. Foster unknowingly picked a popular time of year to leave: right around Easter. Rather than signaling resurrection and renewal, however, leaving close to that holiday gave Southerners unaccustomed to Northern winters time to acclimate before the cold weather descended. (Wilkerson also notes that Easter and the Fourth of July became common times for those who moved North to make return visits South, where their tales and signs of their experiences and opportunities elicited much interest.)

Overground Railroad riders were not victims of circumstance. They may have been both pushed and pulled to the North and the West, but they also exercised their wills. Like others who made long journeys, they demonstrated ambition, determination, resilience and resourcefulness. Certainly disputes arose in black households over whether it was better to stay or go, better to seek freer lives elsewhere or work toward amelioration at home. Such debates could continue, but, without question, leaving the familiar and taking a chance on the unknown required considerable fortitude. It also meant confronting emotionally wrenching dilemmas, like whether to leave behind loved ones, which migrants inevitably did, resulting in what Wilkerson calls "perhaps the greatest single act of family disruption and heartbreak among black Americans in the twentieth century." (This is one reason why large family reunions became popular summertime events in receiving stations like Detroit.) While challenging economic times prompted descendants of some migrants to move back, enduring emotional, cultural and familial bonds certainly had something to do with it as well.

Lawrence, with his bold graphics and blunt accompanying texts, in some respects anticipated the story Wilkerson tells. However, Wilkerson not only offers a more nuanced view; she also corrects earlier versions. She debunks misconceptions about migrants and commonly accepted myths about the Great Migration. Transplants did not uniformly find welcome in the North and West from other blacks; those black-eyed peas did not always have the wished-for effect. ("The Negroes who had been North for quite some time met their fellowmen with disgust and aloofness," Lawrence says of a black couple he shows parading in their finest clothes.) Not all of them were agricultural workers new to urban living. Robert Foster, for instance, was a surgeon barred from operating in the hospital in his hometown who opted to build a medical practice on the Pacific Coast. (He counted Ray Charles among his patients.) Even before Lawrence picked up his brushes, in the 1930s a majority of black migrants in the cities of the North and the West came from cities or towns, not plantations. Often blamed for importing poverty, illiteracy and broken families into black urban communities, the migrants actually were more likely to be employed, earned more, had more education and were more likely to be and to remain married than their Northern-born counterparts, according to Wilkerson's analysis of census records. She attributes these facts to the former Southerners' familiarity with hard times and hard work, willingness to work multiple jobs and long hours, and commitment to improving their lot.

Wilkerson also shows that the standard reasons given for why the Great Migration happened often don't hold up to scrutiny. A cotton-crop decimating boll weevil infestation during the 1920s, a purported cause Lawrence memorializes in pigment and print, can only explain so much. After all, most migrants from Florida, Kentucky, North Carolina, Tennessee, Virginia and west Texas didn't pick cotton to begin with, and many from states where it was the chief industry didn't either. George Starling, for instance, picked citrus fruit before his hasty exit from Florida.

While lynching may have launched migrants on their northern and western trajectories, its role is less straightforward than Lawrence stated. During a forty-year period ending in 1929, someone was burned alive or hanged in the South every four days for such "crimes" as "trying to act like a white person" or insulting one, according to a source Wilkerson cites. Arguing that people were either inured to such brutality or too frightened by it to act, some historians see no causal connection between lynching and black migration from specific areas. Other scholars claim that the evidence does in fact show that such executions did prompt black Southerners to leave. Wilkerson contends that both observations have merit and that lynching most certainly did make potential victims want to relocate, even if they didn't do so immediately. George Starling did go north when a co-worker tipped him off about an imminent lynching, but Ida Mae Gladney and her husband, after deciding to leave because a relative was beaten and jailed for something he didn't do, first finished the cotton-picking season.

Perhaps the Great Migration's impact can best be perceived by trying to imagine what America and the world would be like today if it hadn't occurred. This would have meant that countless shapers of American culture and society might never have existed or might never have become who they became. If Berry Gordy's parents hadn't moved from rural Georgia to Detroit, where he was born, he probably never would have founded Motown and recorded the likes of Diana Ross, whose parents similarly migrated there from the South. Miles Davis, Nat King Cole, Jimi Henrdix, Aretha Franklin, Michael Jackson, John Coltrane, Thelonious Monk and

Whitney Houston might never have been heard from if their parents or grandparents hadn't joined the Great Migration and reared them in the West or the North. Then again, perhaps the model of Memphis, Tennessee-based Stax Records, Motown's rival for rhythm and blues and soul music, would have become more commonplace in the South, and we would have heard from at least some of them in different contexts. (Franklin was born in Memphis, not far from Stax, though her family moved north when she was still quite young.) Throughout much of the 1960s, Stax worked routinely with interracial groups, including its house band, Booker T and the MGs. (When Martin Luther King was assassinated in the city, racial tensions penetrated the recording studio and disrupted its racial harmony.) Then still again, perhaps Southern cities would have become the hotbeds of black cultural life that locales like Harlem and, for a time, Detroit, actually became.

Music is hardly the only area where this thought experiment applies. Wilkerson names writers such as Toni Morrison, August Wilson, James Baldwin and Richard Wright (from whom she borrows her title); athletes like Joe Louis, Venus and Serena Williams, Jesse Owens and basketball great Bill Russell (whose parents hailed from Dr. Foster's hometown); and celebrated strivers including Oprah Winfrey, Condoleezza Rice, Bill Cosby, Michelle Obama and Spike Lee. The earliest black men to become mayors of major U.S. cities – such as Cleveland's Carl Stokes, Los Angeles's Tom Bradley and Detroit's Coleman Young – came from families that participated in the Great Migration. Would Southern cities have been the first to be led by such men if circumstances hadn't pushed their families north? Or would they instead have become fertile ground for the black political separation movement of the 1960s, perhaps as white residents instead fled, much as they did from some northern cities as black migrants moved into them? Such counterfactual speculation is tricky, of course. So much would have been different for the Great Migration *not* to have occurred that the country would already have been a very different place. But trying to imagine possible scenarios brings home just how far-reaching the changes caused by the Great Migration truly were.

Wilkerson could have supplied many, many more examples. She might have mentioned Florida-born Ossian Sweet, who, after earning his medical degree at Howard University, settled in Detroit, where, two days after Labor Day, 1925, an all-white, rock-throwing "neighborhood improvement association" attempted to expel him from the house he and his wife had just purchased. Sweet's brother fired a rifle from a bedroom window, killing a man outside. The family's armed self-defense led to a high-profile murder trial with famed "attorney for the damned" Clarence Darrow arguing the Sweets' case. The Sweets' act (and the NAACP's efforts to publicize it and pay their attorney) ultimately helped undermine the racist housing restrictions many migrants confronted in the North. Surprisingly, Wilkerson also does not name Jacob Lawrence himself, who might not have won recognition for his migration series and become the first African-American artist to have work in the permanent collection of the Museum of Modern Art if his family, which came from South Carolina and Virginia, hadn't moved north.

Of course, the Great Migration also produced sharecroppers-turned-factory workers like Ida Mae Gladney, railroad porters like George Starling and physicians like Robert Foster as well as teachers, autoworkers and store clerks. Although economic enticement in the form of a labor shortage in the North helped start the "leaderless revolution," as Wilkerson aptly terms it, these migrants also sought emancipation from segregationist repression. Wilkerson likens their "mass act of independence" to immigrants crossing the Atlantic Ocean and the Rio Grande—with the key difference being that black Southerners sought their rights within their own country. For that reason she regards the story she tells in *The Warmth of Other Suns* as both distinctly American and universal.

The migrants' quest for material advantages and political freedom was never solely about geography, and population churning persisted. Even before the conclusion of the Great Migration in 1970, some ex-Southerners considered going back, and this desire often intensified toward the end of their lives as they contemplated being buried beside their deceased elders back home. (Wilkerson touches on reverse migration only briefly.) Some had wanted to secure superior circumstances for their children and grandchildren, many of whom later decided to return to the Old Country, which had become a very different place than the one their ancestors left. While Lawrence might never have envisioned black Americans going back to the South, their doing so actually shows how profoundly the Great Migration altered the nation. The transformation of the South into a desirable destination just might work as the logical next chapter of this ongoing story.

NINTH INTERLUDE

Although Americans celebrate the Fourth of July because of its association with a famous document, what transpired with Thomas Jefferson's celebrated words cannot be accurately assigned to a single day. The Continental Congress adopted a resolution calling for a break from Great Britain on the second day of the month. It did endorse the final, edited version of the Declaration of Independence two days later. The holiday thus marks an administrative gesture, the formalization of a decision already made, which few people knew about at the time. Official copies of the Declaration were not printed for another two weeks and it was not signed until early August 1776. Further, Philadelphia newspapers first reported the story on July 6. General George Washington's troops heard that the colonies had been pronounced "Free and Independent States" two days later. When Joseph J. Ellis says in American Creation *that the Declaration of Independence was "sent out to the world on July 4, 1776," he quietly ignores that the world did not receive it until later. No one actually celebrated the Fourth of July in 1776.*

While the Fourth eventually came to be regarded as the country's birthday, that, too, oversimplifies the reality. "There were really two founding moments," Ellis explains: "The first in 1776, which declared American independence, and the second in 1787-88, which declared American nationhood."

If multiple ornamental occasions for the two stages of creation would have been too extravagant and a single date needed to be settled on, then John Adams would say his countrymen went with the wrong one. The nation's second president believed July 2 saw the pivotal event when the Congress passed the resolution calling for independence that Richard Henry Lee of Virginia had moved on June 7. In a letter to his wife, Abigail, he wrote: "The second day of July, 1776, will be the most memo-

rable epocha in the history of America. I am apt to believe that it will be celebrated by succeeding generations as the great anniversary festival." He envisioned precisely the sorts of festivities (including fireworks) that came to surround celebrations held two days later.

Both Jefferson and Adams died on the Declaration's recognized fiftieth anniversary. President John Quincy Adams referred in his diary to the "striking coincidence" of Jefferson dying on July 4. He did not learn for several days that his father died only a few hours after Jefferson, according to historian Sean Wilentz. Adams had the man who succeeded him as president on his mind at the end. His last words were "Thomas Jefferson still lives" or some variation on that line, which was technically incorrect but "right for the ages," in Ellis's assessment. Jefferson had the date rather than Adams in his thoughts, asking immediately before becoming comatose: "Is it the Fourth?"

Adams believed Jefferson's role in the actual decision to declare independence had been overblown; Adams thought he deserved more credit for the move to break with England than he received and that his vice president deserved less. According to Ellis, Adams responded to organizers of the 1826 "Jubilee of Independence" by "insisting that the Fourth of July was not really the right date, indeed there was no one right date, and the passage of the Declaration of Independence was merely an ornamental occasion bereft of any larger historical significance."

In this instance, Adams may have been literally right and the day in 1776 itself carried no real intrinsic importance. However, he missed how fraught with meaning even the most artificial of holidays could become over time. Prizefighter Jack Johnson's Independence Day story, occurring 134 years after the original "wrong" one, illustrates the point.

For me to look at personal identity as I do – that is, as the sum of my own choices – takes no special courage. For others in different circumstances to do so, it did. To disregard and disdain partitions as Johnson did demanded extraordinary bravery.

Arthur John Jackson was born in Galveston, Texas, on March 31, 1878, which was, as his biographer Geoffrey C. Ward points out, one year "after the last Union troops were withdrawn from the former Confederacy, leaving freed blacks to fend for themselves." That's exactly what Johnson did. Throughout his life, he sought freedom from constraint and tried to make every day his Independence Day.

JACK JOHNSON'S FOURTH OF JULY

Of course Jack Johnson and Jim Jeffries fought on the date they did. In retrospect it's hard to think of it happening any other time. A biographer likens Johnson's outlook to the one expressed by the author of the Declaration of Independence, and there's a poetic appropriateness to pairing the fighter and the Founding Father, two uncompromising champions of freedom. There's a wonderful rightness, then, to Johnson's victory over Jeffries occurring on the Fourth of July.

The event contributes another chapter to the holiday's history of contradiction and struggle. From the start, Independence Day honored an unrealized ideal. The country that declared a commitment to liberty denied many residents their freedom. Abolitionists drew attention to the distance between the nation's enshrined principles and the far different reality. William Lloyd Garrison, in an 1829 Fourth of July address, said the holiday was filled with "hypocritical cant about the rights of man." On the same date twenty-five years later, Garrison burned a copy of the slavery-encoding Constitution, which he called a deal with the devil. Frederick Douglass, who fought for the eradication of the "shocking and bloody" practice of slavery, said pre-Civil War Independence Day celebrations exposed the two-facedness of a nation that spoke of liberty while permitting enslavement of others. "This Fourth of July is *yours*, not *mine*," the former slave said. Douglass sought to extend the "rich inheritance of justice, liberty, prosperity and independence" engendered by the Revolution to all people in the country. The Declaration of Independence articulated doctrines that could not justly apply to only certain groups. "In effect," writes historian Eric Foner, "Douglass argued that in their desire for freedom, the slaves were truer to the nation's underlying principles than the white Americans

- 99 -

who annually celebrated the Fourth of July." Garrison suggested that if slaves rebelled, they could find justifications in the Declaration.

The Emancipation Proclamation and the North's victory in the Civil War dramatically altered the meaning of the holiday. Radically different ideas of freedom prevailed in the country's warring halves, according to the president who kept them together. For the North, freedom meant each man being able to enjoy "the product of his labor," while white Southerners took freedom to mean the ability to do "as they please with other men, and the product of other men's labor," said Abraham Lincoln. The ascendancy of one of these definitions made a profound impact. As Foner puts it in *The Story of American Freedom*:

The Union's triumph consolidated the northern understanding of freedom as the national norm. In the process, the meaning of freedom, and the identity of those entitled to enjoy its blessing, were themselves transformed.

The change could be seen in the attitude toward Independence Day among black residents, who finally could claim the day as *theirs*. Black southerners embraced the holiday after the Civil War. Many of their white counterparts, however, refused to celebrate it, according to Foner.

Certainly the outcome of the war did not immediately mean freedom and equality for all. The transformation remained incomplete. One hundred years later – and well after Johnson's death in 1946 – disenfranchised blacks continued to call on the country finally to meet the promises made by the Declaration of Independence. "Like the abolitionists, civil rights activists sought to identify the nation's cherished symbols of freedom with their cause," says Foner. Oppressed people's commitment to the ideals represented by those emblems makes for a very American story.

The story of the racially incendiary boxing match between Johnson and Jeffries and its bloody aftermath is also peculiarly American. The bout carried especially great symbolic weight partially because of the date when it was held and partially because of America's tragic obsession with assigning meaning to pigmentation. The fight had very real nationwide consequences.

In a period when white champions routinely refused to enter the ring with black boxers, Johnson had to chase his predecessor as heavyweight champion, Tommy Burns, around the globe before convincing him to fight in Australia. When Johnson became the first black heavyweight championship in 1908, racists reacted with bloody-minded fury and demanded that the title be reclaimed by a white man. Writer Jack London had rooted for Burns because of tribal allegiance. "He was a white man and so am I," London explained. "Naturally, I want to see the white man win." London called on Jeffries to return to the ring and depose Johnson. Jeffries, a more celebrated boxer than Burns, refused to fight black men once he had won the title in 1899. He retired in 1905 and had taken up farming and other pursuits. Johnson's "golden smile" when he beat Burns especially rankled London. "Jeffries must emerge from his alfalfa farm and remove that smile from Johnson's face," London insisted. Five years after leaving the sport, Jeffries agreed to rise from his pastoral repose and challenge Johnson in the name of white supremacy, stating the day before the fight: "I realize full well what depends on me.... That portion of the white race that has been looking to me to defend its athletic superiority may feel assured that I am fit to do my very best.... I will win as quickly as I can." Fifteen rounds proved that Jeffries could not win, quickly or otherwise.

By beating Jeffries, Johnson cemented his status as the preeminent boxer of the time – and did much more than that. Johnson "was the most dominant force in all of boxing for the first twenty years" of the twentieth century, Arthur Ashe writes in *A Hard Road to Glory*. The tennis star regards Johnson as "the most significant black athlete in history." Muhammad Ali's biographer Thomas Hauser takes a different view.

He believes Ali's individuality and influence make him the true champion of champions. "With or without Jack Johnson, eventually a black man would have won the heavyweight championship of the world," Hauser asserts in *The Lost Legacy of Muhammad Ali*. He goes on to say:

And sooner or later, there would have been a black athlete who, like Joe Louis, was universally admired and loved. But Ali carved out a place in history that was, and remains, uniquely his alone. And it's unlikely that anyone other than Muhammad Ali could have created and fulfilled that role. Ali didn't just mirror his times. He wasn't a passive figure carried along by currents stronger than he was. He fought the current; he swam against the tide. He stood for something, stayed with it, and prevailed.

But Hauser doesn't give Johnson sufficient credit here, and he overlooks similarities between his preferred fighter and Johnson. "The parallels between the two black boxers were striking," Randy Roberts points out in *Papa Jack: Jack Johnson and the Era of the White Hopes* – "both confronted legal authority, both suffered through periods of exile, and both were great showmen in and out of the ring."

As a boxer, Johnson was ahead of his time. He was inventive, developing a fighting style closer to that of contemporary fighters than that of his peers. Indeed, he closely resembles Ali, who during his rise to the championship frequently weathered criticism for rejecting a conventional approach and insisting on boxing (and living) his own way. Again like Ali, Johnson demeaned his opponents and appeared to enjoy humiliating them – or at least the white ones (while Ali insulted fellow blacks). And doing *what* he did *when* he did made a difference. "Within the United States," Ashe insists, "Jack Johnson had a larger impact than Ali because he was the first. Nothing that any African-American had done up until that time had the same impact as Jack Johnson's fight against James Jeffries."

Johnson's firsts were not confined to athletic achievement alone. When he signed on to the Jeffries fight, which was originally slated to occur in San Francisco rather than Reno, the contract "constituted the largest legitimate business deal ever consummated by an African-American to that time," according to Ashe. Johnson also earned what may have been the largest amount of money a black American had ever made in a single day until that point: $121,000. He enjoyed the fruits of his labor on an unprecedented scale. He did so as a self-proclaimed "pure-blooded American" whose enslaved ancestors had been taken to the land where he was born "before the United States was dreamed of." In a letter, Thomas Jefferson wrote that "the mass of mankind has not been born with saddles on their backs, nor a favored few booted and spurred, ready to ride them legitimately, by the grace of God." Throughout his life, Johnson refused to wear a saddle on his broad back. Instead, he "resolved to live always as if color did not exist," as Geoffrey C. Ward describes the boxer's approach in *Unforgivable Blackness: The Rise and Fall of Jack Johnson.* "I have found no better way of avoiding race prejudice than to act with people of other races as if prejudice did not exist," the fighter says in one of his autobiographies. Though fully aware of the significance others attached to skin color, he wanted a color-blind world and tried to live as if he resided in one.

Johnson's defeat of the Great White Hope Jeffries provided ample evidence of racial prejudice's continued existence, and many of his fans could not avoid its pernicious consequences. As news of Johnson's victory spread around the nation, so did celebrations in black neighborhoods, which in turn were met with violence. "Rioting broke out like prickly heat all over the country between whites sore and angry that Jeffries had lost the big fight at Reno and negroes jubilant that Johnson had won," the *New York Tribune* reported the day after the fight. A black marching band in New Orleans had to run from bricks thrown by men incensed at the idea of the title belt circling a non-white waist. In Houston, a white streetcar passenger slit the throat of a black fan who cheered for Johnson. A black motorist was stopped and lynched in Wheeling, West Virginia, and in Georgia white shooters killed three black construction workers and injured five more. Between eleven and twenty six people were killed and hundreds more were injured; most of them were black. "No event since emancipation forty-five years earlier seemed to mean so much to Negro America as Johnson's victory," writes Ward, who ranks the fight's aftermath as one of the most intense episodes of nationwide racial violence in the twentieth century before the assassination of Martin Luther King, Jr., almost six decades later.

Johnson himself could not avoid the dangers of blood-thinking he so wanted to ignore. The United States federal government, deliberately misapplying the White Slave Traffic Act (also known as the Mann Act) and depending on the dubious story of a prostitute, constructed a transparently unjust criminal case in an effort to destroy Johnson, which initially drove him into exile but ultimately resulted in his spending a year in prison. Even if he did confront forces larger and stronger than he was, Johnson can't be considered an unresisting victim of history. Even if Johnson did not strive to advance a cause other than himself, as Ali did, his determined rejection of limitations did make a difference. Even if, as Roberts correctly states, Johnson "was not a doctrinaire revolutionary" and "his ethics were akin to those of a circus barker," by his actions he dared his country to meet its promise of liberty for all.

Long before Muhammad Ali pointed to his own appearance as evidence of the beauty of blackness or Joe Louis simultaneously knocked out Max Schmeling and fantasies of white supremacy associated with the German fighter, Johnson challenged entrenched racial myths. Johnson's disregard for prevailing notions of what a black man ought to do –whether winning a prestigious sporting prize or marrying a white woman (as he did multiple times) – threatened certain people and encouraged others.

When he became the second black heavyweight champion, Louis set out to redo – and, to an extent, to undo – what Johnson had done. He did so by consciously adopting a less divisive, controversial persona. Early on, his handlers "spread a kind of 'official' image of Louis's character that strongly influenced public perceptions of Louis for the rest of his career," writes biographer Chris Mead. "They wanted to dissociate Louis from the memory of Jack Johnson." Louis was directed not to gloat after knocking down an opponent. Outside the ring, he did not brag; he complimented opponents instead. He avoided being photographed with white women. He was presented as a "model of middle-class virtue" as far removed from "Johnson's negative image as possible." The careful construction of his image had the desired result. Prior to World War II, white sportswriters "had emphasized the differences between Louis and themselves by stereotyping him, referring to his color, calling him a 'credit to his race' and 'an African,'" Mead says in *Champion: Joe Louis – Black Hero in White America*. Subsequently, they followed the example of newspaperman Jimmy Cannon by repeating the line that Louis was "a credit to his race – meaning not the colored race, but the human race," and by explicitly identifying Louis as an American.

Johnson can also be seen as the embodiment of American principles, even if in his day and for decades afterward, he looked to some like a threat to the social order. "The world belongs to the living," Roberts writes in *Papa Jack*. "It had been Thomas Jefferson's philosophy and it was Jack Johnson's." For Johnson, living meant freedom from constraint. Behaving as though he was unbound by race, by insisting on the human right to equality and independence, he challenged the contemporary standards of white America and the approach of cautious reformers. He was, in his reckless way, truer to the nation's foundational premises than those who didn't think they held true for all people. The boxer's supporters and detractors did not fit into discrete skin-color-defined camps.

Booker T. Washington, for instance, refrained from reveling in Johnson's athletic success and despised his ostentatious lifestyle, with its flashy clothes, fast cars and long parade of sexual partners. Washington denounced Johnson for "misrepresenting the colored people of this country."

But Johnson never wanted to be anybody's representative. "The champion refused to consider himself a symbol," Roberts points out. "He was man, a free man, this and nothing more." He didn't present himself as a spokesman for his race (the way Jeffries, or later, Ali did). "He did just as *he* pleased," as Roberts phrases it. He aimed to enjoy precisely what America purported to be all about: the unfettered exercise of equal opportunity. Looked at from a certain perspective, he could be taken as a rebel against the racism he regularly confronted. Yet even as large portions of the U.S. population reviled him, Johnson also fit the national archetype. Johnson regarded himself as quintessentially American, and he tried to make the nation's most cherished symbol of freedom his own by wearing an American flag as a belt when he fought Jeffries. "He was in the great American tradition of self-invented men, too," writes Ward. "All his life, whites and blacks alike would ask him, 'Just who do you think you are?' The answer, of course, was always 'Jack Johnson.'"

Jack Johnson cared foremost and perhaps only about his own independence. According to Ward, "nothing – no law or custom, no person white or black, male or female – could keep him for long from what he wanted." And what he wanted was freedom for himself. This simple idea had a revolutionary aspect and a symbolic resonance whether he wished for it or not. So it is fitting that Johnson made his impact in large part because of what he did on the Fourth of July. He made it *his.* An event intended to convey one meaning about the country and who should represent it ended up doing something altogether different. Though the fight's stagers may have hoped Jefferies would handily remove a man they saw as an illegitimate interloper into a white man's preserve, Johnson's win boldly disrupted plans in an ironic reversal with the force of revelation. Johnson was "determined to live according to his own rules," Roberts writes. "As his smile suggested, his life was his own, he meant to enjoy it, and he did not give a damn what anyone else thought." And what, I ask you, could be more American than that?

TENTH INTERLUDE

Jack Johnson may have tried to live as if racial and ethnic backgrounds didn't matter, but, as I discuss in "Partitions on Parade," many other boxers and fight fans adamantly insist on their enduring importance. And what, I could have asked, is more American than that?

Well, how about shoehorning religion into the secular fiestas? If that's not uniquely American, it sure is frequently seen in the United States.

IRONIES ON PARADE

Growing up in Detroit gave me the sense of irony an appreciation of Labor Day demands. Back when there were still automobile industry jobs to be had in the city, members of the United Auto Workers and other unions would start marching on two separate boulevards that converged downtown, where the dual flanks would merge, as if to symbolize labor's gathering force. That part of town would always be desolate on weekends, so few spectators would see this act of collective wishful thinking. One year when I lived near part of the parade route I wandered over to watch. This would have been between my brief stints in the United Food and Commercial Workers (as a grocery store bagboy during high school) and the National Writers Union (UAW Local 1981), which I joined when I resided in New York after I (like so many others) left Detroit. Someone handed me a sign and I ended up joining in for a while, walking past closed businesses facing empty sidewalks. The placard concerned a specific struggle involving a union, and an industry, other than my own. Carrying it felt faintly fraudulent. Marching alone in the Labor Day parade, with no banner to stand behind or organization to represent, didn't feel like solidarity. I gave my sign to someone who belonged to a group and made my way back home.

The ironies of Labor Day go much deeper than my ambivalent personal experiences with it as someone from a place where the waxing and waning of organized labor's power are a massive part of local history. The ironies – and there are several – reach to the holiday's very roots. One is a relatively minor matter of date selection. Local celebrations of workers' collective strength in the United States predated the declaration of May Day, their international equivalent. While May

- 109 -

Day itself never took a firm hold in the United States, the first day of May's selection for a global event resulted from the earlier scheduling of an American event. Others have deeper significance. As discussed below, the U.S. president who made Labor Day a national holiday did so soon after sending federal forces to end a major strike, precisely the maneuver he'd opposed while campaigning for office around the time of another labor action with a bloody ending. The leader whose union that president decimated had initially backed his electoral campaign. For his involvement in the strike, the unionist ended up in jail, from which he emerged as a national figure who became one of the most prominent third party presidential candidates in the nation's history. May Day and Labor Day share decidedly secular origins, but workers saw religious elements grafted onto their holidays. Unions in the city that first celebrated Labor Day eventually saw their members preferring to use the day off from work that their efforts won for activities other than a parade, which they eventually held on another day, if at all.

The convocation of socialist parties and unions known as the Second International in 1889 passed a resolution calling for a simultaneous, worldwide demonstration in favor of laws limiting the working day to eight hours. Since such a rally had already been planned in the United States for the following May 1, the body decided to use that date. As it fell on a Thursday, unions in various countries found themselves having to decide whether members should go on strike in support of the cause. Cautious parties and unions opted to demonstrate on the first Sunday of the month instead. However, historian Eric Hobsbawm insists that refusing to work made May Day meaningful. In a paper on it in *Uncommon People* (1998), he writes:

> It was the act of symbolically stopping work which turned May Day into more than just another demonstration, or even another commemorative occasion.... For refraining from work on a working day

- 110 -

was both an assertion of working-class power – in fact, the quintessential assertion of this power – and the essence of freedom, namely not being forced to labour in the sweat of one's brow, but choosing what to do in the company of family and friends. It was thus both a gesture of class assertion and class struggle and a holiday: a sort of trailer for the good life to come after the emancipation of labour.

The call for this symbolically potent event did not specify it as a recurring one, but with the day's success, in the form of unexpectedly high levels of participation in many cities, the Brussels International Socialist Congress of 1891 pledged that May Day should be celebrated every year. By the time of its centenary, May Day qualified as an official holiday in more than 100 countries.

The holiday's symbolism extends beyond the act of stopping work. "Spring holidays are profoundly rooted in the ritual cycle of the year in the temperate northern hemisphere," observes Hobsbawm, "and indeed the month of May itself symbolizes the renewal of nature." Flowers figured prominently in celebrations from the very start. Indeed, May Day celebrations of seasonal renewal happened long before an organized labor movement seized the day. Even then the day involved symbolism relating to both economic class and seasonal renewal. For example, during Shakespeare's lifetime, according to scholar Stephen Greenblatt, "on May Day people had long celebrated the legend of Robin Hood, with raucous, often bawdy rituals" involving dancing around a Maypole "decked with ribbons and garlands" and a young Queen of the May also decorated with flowers. One of the most popular May Day icons depicts a Phrygian bonnet-wearing girl amid garlands.

Before May Day blossomed internationally, autumn Labor Day celebrations started in New York City, gradually spreading to other areas. "Ironically, in the USA itself May Day was never to establish itself as it did elsewhere, if only because an

- 111 -

increasingly official holiday of labour, Labor Day, the first Monday in September, was already in existence," explains Hobsbawm. At that time, however, it did not exist as a holiday throughout the country. The Central Labor Union organized the first Labor Day in New York on September 5, 1882. After celebrating it again on the same date the next year, the union picked the first weekday of the month as the time for the "workingmen's holiday" in subsequent years and urged other cities to do so as well. Although the New York unionists' creation effectively kept May Day from catching on in the United States, holiday imagery connects the city with the international festival: a German plaque commemorating the first May Day represents the Statue of Liberty on one side and Karl Marx on the other.

Early local Labor Day events included calls for the establishment of a national holiday, which happened in 1894, immediately after the movement suffered a shattering defeat. Specifically, President Glover Cleveland signed the bill just days after the end of a massive strike against the Pullman Palace Car Company in Illinois. That labor action became named for its leading unionist. Cleveland was responding to protests against his aggressive tactics to suppress what became called the "Debs Rebellion." Eugene Debs led the American Railway Union, which had come into being less than a year before Pullman workers, angered both by severe wage cuts and by the firing of three men who had presented management with a list of grievances, put down their tools. Not only did they stop building Pullman sleeping cars; they and railroad workers around the country (against Debs's advice) began a boycott of any railroad that continued to pull them, refusing to run any train with one attached. The boycott went into effect on June 25 and by the end of the month almost 125,000 workers joined it, affecting twenty railroads. "Across the nation the American Railway Union was so successful during the first week that the old Knights of Labor slogan, 'An injury to one is the concern of all,' seemed fulfilled, as yet another impressive display of labor unity spread throughout the country," writes Nick Salvatore in *Eugene V. Debs: Citizen and Socialist* (1984). Union members' muscle-flexing aggravated and worried management, which aimed to dismantle Debs's young union and its brand of militancy. The railroad corporations' General Managers Association persuaded the federal government that the strike disrupted mail delivery and impeded interstate commerce. Judges issued an injunction against Debs and the union on these grounds and Cleveland (against Governor John Altgeld's advice) agreed to send troops to enforce it. The troops arrived the evening before Independence Day.

When campaigning for the presidency in 1892, Cleveland had opposed the use of federal troops to squelch a strike that summer, one that ultimately saw private enforcers shooting strikers (with a few of their own being killed as well). After strikers took over the Carnegie steelworks in Homestead, Pennsylvania, the company hired "watchmen" from the Pinkerton Protective Patrol to wrest control back from the workers. Started as a private detective agency, the Pinkertons increasingly focused on protecting industry's interests after the death of founder Allan Pinkerton, in 1884, when his son Robert took power. "Over two decades," reports J. Anthony Lukas in *Big Trouble* (1997), "the agency intervened in some seventy strikes, often with violent consequences." This was the case in Homestead, where a gun fight between Pinkertons and strikers resulted in ten deaths and dozen of injuries.

Debs backed Cleveland for the presidency then, encouraged by his position on the strike again Carnegie, but the president's move two years later spurred his radicalization. The strike destroyed his union, which, after membership plummeted, formally disbanded in 1897. Arrested on charges of conspiracy and contempt of court relating to the injunction, Debs later served a six-month sentence, during which (according to the legend Debs helped to cultivate) he converted to socialism. In the related trials, Clarence Darrow defended him, prompting the attorney's lifelong commitment to the cause of organized labor. Roughly a decade later, Darrow would defend labor leaders accused of commissioning murder, including the secretary-treasurer of the Western Federation of Miners, William "Big Bill" Haywood, whom Lukas said "probably ranked with Eugene V. Debs – the lanky labor organizer form Indiana who now headed the Socialist Party of America – as the most feared radicals in the land." Debs would ultimately run for president five times on the ticket of the party he helped to launch. In 1912, Debs won a respectable six percent of the national presidential vote, the highest level ever charted by a national Socialist candidate.

Beyond its impact on Debs's political outlook and activity, the Pullman strike was a pivotal historical event revealing great tensions in American society. Lukas calls it "the largest concerted labor action in the nation's history." Debs thought it was something even bigger than that. In his assessment, Cleveland's decision to send troops changed the event from a strike against railroad corporations "into a conflict in which the organized forces of society and all the powers of the municipal, State and Federal governments were arraigned against us [i.e., workers]." It brought class struggle out into the open. Two Pullman strikers were shot to death by deputy marshals enforcing the will of the corporations. A desire to mollify workers outraged by his handling of the incidents outside Chicago certainly lay behind Cleveland's signing on to the Labor Day holiday.

In effect, then, Labor Day became a holiday as a consequence of a labor movement setback. After the strike, Pullman employees agreed not to unionize. The destruction of his union prompted Debs to pursue leadership of a political movement that also ended in failure, if measured in terms of actual electoral success or in the fomenting of a revolution. The holiday endured as time for parades or picnics, but not in anything like the form its early advocates envisioned. That is, not as a piston in an engine of social change.

The Pullman strike highlighted strife within the labor

movement, dramatically displaying competing conceptions of its aims and methods as represented by Debs and his rival Samuel Gompers. "One of American history's grandest ironies is the role of labor leaders: through their lives and careers can be traced the fascinating pursuit of a perennial ideal, international solidarity for working class advancement and a cooperative society – thrown in reverse," Paul Buhle writes in *Taking Care of Business* (1999). He regards Samuel Gompers as precisely such a figure. Buhle calls Gompers the principal architect of "business unionism," in which the organizations operate just like corporations, including the bestowal of perks for executives, with the goal of labor's emancipation forgotten. Gompers opposed the formation of Debs's American Railway Union, calling it "the disruptive movement." Preferring stability, Gompers, who founded the American Federation of Labor in 1886, aimed to organize the movement on business principles and concentrated on security for skilled workers. Consequently, the AFL "was sometimes regarded as a league of petit-bourgeois tradesmen seeking to protect their status from challenges by the industrialized masses," says Lukas.

Debs aligned himself with the very masses Gompers disdained. "While there is a lower class, I am in it; while there is a criminal element, I am of it; while there is a soul in prison, I am not free," he proclaimed after being convicted in 1918 of violating the Espionage Act by speaking in support of jailed opponents of U.S. intervention in World War I. (President Warren Harding pardoned Debs on Christmas day, 1921.) Debs conceived of unions as having a much greater purpose than attaining higher pay for certain skilled workers. He believed the organization of unions on an industrial basis rather than as separate trades or crafts gave all workers greater strength. He had aimed to organize all railroad workers because he saw earlier strikes fail due to rivalries between or lack of cooperation among various railroad craft unions. He viewed Gompers as a traitor to the labor movement cause and referred to the AFL as a group of "labor-dividing-and-corruption-breeding craft unions." (Just as Gompers refused to back the American Railway Union, he later came into conflict with the Western Federation of Miners. When the WFM president visited Debs soon before the union withdrew from the AFL, the two bonded over their mutual Gompers-related grievances, according to Lukas.) Debs regarded unions as agents for the complete transformation of society, not as mere special interest groups existing within and enforcing hierarchical social structures.

In other historical ironies, it was the AFL that organized the demonstration in May that ended up determining the date of the worldwide workers' holiday in 1890, and, after Pullman, industrial unions like the American Railway Union foundered or disintegrated, while the AFL carried on using the business unionism model. Put another way, an organization that once (at least indirectly) spurred aggressive unionism later opted for a much more timid approach.

Deep divides over the meaning of the labor movement and its symbolic expression also emerged in Labor Day activities. Some New York unions viewed with ambivalence the routine of marching along Fifth Avenue, with what they interpreted as its opulent displays of capitalists' wealth. Early in the twentieth century, certain labor organizations refused to join in the parade along the "avenue of enemies." One militant proposed a "charge up Fifth Avenue with axes and swords." Some even encouraged May Day marches as alternatives to Labor Day traditions. At one, Elizabeth Gurley Flynn, as president of the Socialistic Women of Greater New York, addressed demonstrators in Union Square, saying, "We have not marched today as labor does on Labor Day. Then it goes up Fifth Avenue and is reviewed like so many cattle by the forces of capital. Today we review ourselves and note our own power."

These activists sought to celebrate a power with a material rather than spiritual foundation. While people around the world have numerous religious holidays in common, non-religious ones have not been so widely adopted. May

Day provided an exception. Hobsbawm says it "is perhaps the only unquestionable dent made by a secular movement in the Christian or any other official calendar." (With that "perhaps" he allows for the possibility that nonreligious holidays like Veterans Day could have a claim to the distinction he bestows on May Day, while specifying the involvement of a "movement" narrows the field of possible claimants to the distinction.)

Nevertheless, the workers' holiday does have a spiritual side, and did so from the start. Hobsbawm recognizes this: "The similarity of the new socialist movement to a religious movement, even, in the first heady years of May Day, to a religious revival movement with messianic expectations was patent." Italian socialists called the new holiday "the workers' Easter." A Belgian pamphlet containing what the historian calls a May Day sermon bears epigraphs attributed to both Marx and Jesus.

Also in Belgium, the Christian Labor Movement organized annual commemorations of the papal encyclical *Rerum Novarum* during the Feast of the Ascension as an alternative to the red-tinged May Day. *Rerum Novarum,* which Pope Leo XIII issued in 1891, also recognized some parallels between the labor movement and Catholicism and sought to harness the former to the latter by endorsing the right to organize while simultaneously defending private property as a matter of natural law. The letter to bishops advised that employers should recognize each worker as "a person ennobled by Christian character" and warned that the "rich should tremble at the threatenings of Jesus Christ," which is not quite how Marx would have phrased it.

And that, of course, was precisely the point. The encyclical purporting to codify the "Rights and Duties of Labor and Capital" in essence sought to defuse any revolutionary ardor among workers and to fortify the superior position of employers. While asserting the dignity of labor, the Church clearly hoped to keep workers in the fold and apart from secular movements. It also aimed to forestall fundamental changes in power relations. Suffering, including economic hardship, is an ineradicable part of human existence, *Rerum Novarum* counsels, and workers should accept this and not expect or pursue equality. While organizing for somewhat better wages and working conditions might be okay, it allows, unions shouldn't go too far, since private ownership of property is enshrined in natural law, and the social order should not be disrupted. It simultaneously expressed pro-worker sentiments while firmly situating the Church on the side of the status quo.

Though typical of the Catholic Church's duplicitous economic teachings, *Rerum Novarum* was by no means the only Vatican document to lend aid to opponents of the labor movement. Even as the Church expressed support for freedom, in Spain, for example, it operated as an instrument of oppression. It actively supported General Francisco Franco's suppression of workers' freedom of organization. When Franco achieved his final victory over the forces of the Second Republic in 1939, Pope Pius XII thanked him for the "Catholic victory" and bestowed his blessing. Franco was a faithful churchgoer and though it might not have been completely comfortable with every aspect of his regime, the church supported him because he represented a return to Catholic power after the defeat of the secularist Republicans. (Among the many ways Franco's dictatorship and Catholicism intertwined was the power, granted to the Vatican under a 1953 agreement with the Spanish government, to select the country's holidays.) Pius XII's 1931 encyclical *Reconstructing the Social Order* offered a moral basis for fascism in Italy under Benito Mussolini as well as in Spain. It declared socialism incompatible with Catholicism, and Franco invoked the encyclical to justify smashing trade unions once he seized power. It was a reciprocal arrangement: he relied on the church's authority to impose fascism, and the church gave him its support. It approved the state syndicate system, which denied workers of the right to organize independent unions or choose their own representatives. The church was also permitted to operate its own social organizations and related propaganda activities. As Paul Blanshard writes in *Freedom and Catholic Power in Spain and Portugal* (1962), the Catholic Church in Spain worked as "a sustaining partner in the whole economic scheme of repression and control." These encyclicals, and the resulting realities when the church was given the power to implement its economic ideas, show why the irony of nonreligious holidays taking on religious components is much more than a minor nuisance for unbelievers.

Although Labor Day, like May Day, began as a worldly holiday, religion infiltrated it early on. Indeed, if the Pullman strike precipitated the formalization of the secular holiday, the event did have distinct religious overtones. Debs asserted that the workers withholding their labor in support of Pullman employees "advocated and practiced the Christ-like virtue of sympathy." Debs was not shy about assuming something of a messianic role. His biographer likens Debs's style of speaking to preaching. Salvatore also describes the railroad workers who voted to boycott Pullman cars in an effort to combat corporate power as holding their convictions with "religious fervor." Further, "messianic expectations" could be observed in the 100,000 supporters chanting "Debs, Debs, Debs" who greeted him when he left the Woodstock, Illinois, jail, says Salvatore. Although not a religious man, Clarence Darrow described Debs as possessing the very qualities Debs himself viewed as Christ-like. The lawyer said: "There may have lived sometime, somewhere a kindlier, gentler, more generous man than Eugene Victor Debs, but I have never known him." Like the May Day proponents who invoked Jesus in their literature, Debs too relied on scripture, attributing competition to Cain in contradiction to the teaching of Christ, for instance. His rival's organization also found religion in labor's cause. In 1909, the American Federation of Labor declared the Sunday preceding the holiday "Labor Sunday," which it devoted to the spiritual side of the movement. A century later, the AFL-

CIO's website included a page dedicated to "Labor in the Pulpits," with information on the link between faith and workers' rights.

The story of Debs's "conversion" to socialism also entails religious components. Salvatore questions the idea of his having immediately and surely realized the flaws of capitalism and the solution of socialism and the narrative's parallel to Saul's sudden insight on the road to Damascus. He also recognizes that Debs himself promoted the legend. Many years after the strike, Debs claimed he knew little of socialism prior to Pullman but had been "baptized in Socialism in the roar of conflict ... in the gleam of every bayonet and the flash of every rifle *the class struggle was revealed.*" In jail, he said, he studied Marx and others and came out a completely new person. Debs, Salvatore insists, never really followed any orthodox socialist theory and owed much of his thinking to Jefferson and Lincoln rather than Marx. He opened his first speech after walking out of jail in Illinois by referring to the Declaration of Independence, not *The Communist Manifesto.* Still, the legend of a jailhouse conversion and Debs's own commitment to it point to what Salvatore calls the "religious underpinnings of American culture" in his thought. Although the labor movement struggled to improve conditions in this world, it borrowed figures of speech related to otherworldly dreams. It adapted symbols and rhetorical gestures that many, including Debs, believed ennobled the cause, lending it a grandeur and resonance they could not otherwise find language to articulate.

Since the choice of time for a festival has great symbolic import, the suggestiveness of picking a fall day instead of a day in spring is especially striking, hinting at decline and decay from the very beginning of the holiday's observance. The New York Central Labor Council in 2007 cancelled the Labor Day Parade, citing small attendance by participants as well as spectators. Years earlier, the body shifted the parade from Labor Day itself to the following weekend, leaving union members free to do something more appealing with their summer-ending three-day weekend. A century and a quarter after workers took unpaid time off their jobs to insist on the recognition of their holiday, their descendants decided they could dispense with the parade exhibiting "the strength and *esprit de corps* of the trade and labor organizations" called for in the first proposal for Labor Day. They would hold on to the time for holiday festivities, but drop the class assertion. Perhaps they had little choice. Far from signaling the achievement of the post-emancipation "good life," the decision reflected the diminished condition of organized labor in the United States, where union membership fell from almost 50 percent in the 1950s to about 12 percent by 2007. According to *The Chief*, the civil service employees' newspaper, some officials expressed "relief" over the cancellation, saying the parade "had felt more like an annoying family obligation than a celebration of workers' power" and conceding that it no longer served to display working-class solidarity or strength. The muscle that worried management at the end of the nineteenth century had atrophied by the early twenty-first. Although no parade crept down Fifth Avenue, the Labor Day celebration of mass proceeded as usual at Saint Patrick's Cathedral. (The Labor Council resurrected the parade subsequently.)

The history of Labor Day, in addition to involving a surplus of ironies, also disproves an oft spoken cliché. In 1912 (the year Debs won nearly one million votes in his run for the presidency), Darrow spoke in San Francisco on Labor Day. He said it was the first time he'd marched in a parade and that he did not care for it. It made him tired. He disliked walking in the dust but did not want to ride while others walked. His biographers, Arthur and Lila Weinberg, say he was joking. Even so, Darrow, the skeptical lawyer who considered holidays to be "hollow days" hints at what the fate of Labor Day in New York City confirms: not everyone loves a parade. Darrow didn't. I know just how he felt, though my aversion doesn't stem from the physical discomfort of such events. Rather, I can't muster the spirit parade lovers seem to have, and I can't overlook the ironies they seem not to see. Since that long-ago parade in which I briefly shuffled along, I returned to the city where I grew up after many years elsewhere. As far as I know, two distinct, virtually unwatched groups of workers still march down Michigan and Woodward Avenues before joining up in downtown Detroit. I haven't gone to see for myself, and I certainly haven't agreed to carry someone else's sign.

ELEVENTH INTERLUDE

Sometimes, as with Labor Day, religion's intrusion can cause headshaking. It's superfluous, even if it no longer does immediate, obvious, measurable harm (the way the Falange-Vatican alliance in Spain did). Or, as with Easter, it offers fraudulent consolation for deep fears and false answers to real questions. Other times it has far more dire effects. The danger lies in a perverse way of thinking inseparable from religious certitude – the conviction that one can possess divine truth and, therefore, license to impose its strictures on others – or to obliterate nonbelievers. Salman Rushdie's Valentine's Day, on which volunteers in a god's army sought to murder an individual and some of his associates, provided a preview for a larger scale onslaught that occurred a dozen years later. A holiday expresses a group's cherished beliefs and values through actions. September 11, 2001, did that too.

ONE HUNDRED AND TEN BOXES

I.

The date did not do it. We did not leave New York when we did because of what happened there precisely seven years earlier. September 11, 2008, was a Thursday, the day of the week that alternate side of the street parking opened space on what for several years had been our side of the street. Street-cleaning-related rules briefly created an opening for a large truck to stop near a building in need of emptying. For people moving, such practical matters take precedence over symbolism.

While logistical considerations guided our relocation schedule-making, the date did intrude on our thoughts. After our belongings had been hauled away, my wife, Nancy, and I went and sat at John F. Kennedy airport waiting to board our flight to the other side of the country. The required display to uniformed agents of plastic bags containing circumscribed quantities of toiletries, the shuffle through metal detectors on shoeless feet, and the other rituals of security implemented early in the twenty-first century – these alone would have provided plenty of reminders of what day it was. After one of our earlier, exploratory trips to Portland, Oregon, we discovered that the guardians of air transportation in New York had permitted us to carry a knife onto the plane. Swiss Army knives had been a regular part of our travel gear back when flyers did not have to consider the condition of their socks, whether they had more than three ounces of shampoo, or if they had eminently useful combinations of bottle and can opener, food slicer and repair kit in their carry-on luggage. We had not intended to bring the versatile tool with us; it had simply been left in a bag routinely and forgotten until we discovered it while unpacking in the hotel. Nancy had bought this particular knife in Switzerland when we lived there. Rather than test whether Oregon's luggage X-rayers were more diligent than their New York counterparts and risk losing the souvenir, we mailed it back east.

We changed coasts in presidential campaign season. September 11 had become the kind of day on which public figures stand at flag-flanked podiums and say solemn things. The televisions hanging from ceilings throughout the airport terminal broadcast the joint hand-shaking and picture-taking event candidates Barack Obama and John McCain staged where the Twin Towers had stood for almost thirty years. The political rivals walked together in the afternoon sun at what for many years had been a massive concrete lined hole.

We had been past the same void ourselves, though we never deliberately went to look at the devastation. Our first close-up glimpse of the mass-murder site had been inadvertent. We were not making any sort of pilgrimage when we exited a subway station and found ourselves looking at homemade signs posted on every available upright surface near that hole. They showed pictures of the missing whom others still had hope, then, of finding alive. We had an out-of-town visitor who wanted to see something else in that part of lower Manhattan, and, in another case of the practical trumping the symbolic, we had simply taken the most direct route to get there. Another time, we had not asked the livery cab driver to take us through that part of town on the way from Brooklyn to the airport in Newark, New Jersey, but that was the route he chose, making sure we would think about the still-recent catastrophe on our first post-September 11 flight. We would have thought about it anyway, I'm sure.

We did not avoid the World Trade Center zone out any sort of indifference or callousness. Rather, it had not been an area we frequented when the complex existed. We knew people who worked there. During our time living in the city, I had been inside the building only twice, I think, and even then I had not gone up inside either tower. Once I simply went underneath to reach a train. The World Trade Center formed the only part of the city's storied skyline that we could see from our first apartment in Brooklyn, and that was Nancy's vantage point when I telephoned to tell her what had happened to it that fall morning. Before then, if I happened to look up from my book and gaze out the window, I would notice it when trains crossed the East River on the Manhattan Bridge, but I never thought much about the place until it was gone. There had been a distance, both literally and figuratively, between me and it. The idea of going to see that hole seemed inappropriate, unearned, like visiting the grave of a stranger, or, more accurately, thousands of strangers.

We lived in New York longer after than before the obliteration of the structure and many of its occupants. Much like we did with our first walk past what became known as Ground Zero, we ended up in the city but not because of any particular desire to be there. When in Switzerland, Nancy and I both worked on the same publishing project. Near its completion this involved working in New York. Once we were finished, we found other work and stayed. We did not arrive there as part of a conscious plan and, when we moved into our rented apartment on New Year's Day, we never envisioned it as a permanent home. Just as we had in Geneva, we resided in New York with the knowledge that eventually we would go somewhere else.

II.

The city offered as many reasons to stay as to go, as many reasons to go as to stay. Close-standing subway riders; unknown-but-still-despised neighbors who mercilessly expose other tenants to their noise; sidewalk-blocking, stop-and-go baby stroller pushers; long-leash dog walkers; out-of-step tourists; assertively unaware residents; and geniuses who behave as if keeping the rat population thriving on samplings of the world's cuisines were an urban pastime if not a civic duty – these irritants did not motivate us to leave. Unforgettable concerts in small rooms in TriBeCa, Greenwich Village and the Lower East Side and in stately halls uptown; readings by admired authors; plays and operas at Lincoln Center and the Brooklyn Academy of Music; championship boxing at Madison Square Garden; unsurpassable meals at places within walking distance of our apartment, at Michelin Guide-endorsed restaurants engineered by Thomas Keller, and at tradition-bound steak houses; and the regular exposure to varieties of real genius – these did not persuade us to stay.

New York may offer the world, but it also makes residents want to tune it out. A large number of people in a small amount of space – the very thing that makes the vitality of the city's cultural life possible – encourages willful obliviousness as a way of coping with others' unbearable nearness. Dealing with the inevitable intrusiveness of others this way escalates inconsideration: when almost everyone behaves as if no one else matters, then only the misguided or the saintly willingly act like the sucker who gives a damn. This discourages basic decency (which survives only as an eccentricity noteworthy mainly for its rareness) and promotes humans' worst impulses, including an aggressive, intentional disregard for others. New Yorkers routinely behave as if no one else walks with them on the crowded sidewalk and no one lives on the other side of the wall. Even as it encourages a ceaselessly reinvigorated and reinvigorating cultural bonanza, New York has a coarsening and dulling effect over time.

People need to move away from "the same worn-out soil" in order to thrive, Nathaniel Hawthorne asserts in the passage in "The Custom House" from which Jhumpa Lahiri takes the title of *Unaccustomed Earth,* one of the last books we obtained before imposing a pre-move moratorium. We had responded to the impetus for unsettlement before. One summer before we were married, Nancy and I took two months and drove around the country, traveling almost nine thousand miles through twenty-two states. On a freeway in Arizona we glimpsed the aftermath of a fiery accident involving eighteen-wheelers, including a residential mover's truck, which almost certainly instilled a subsequent wariness over subjecting everything we owned to such a possible end. On our first wedding anniversary, we flew to Switzerland, where a six-month stint at a United Nations agency grew to last for more than a year. While there, we traveled as frequently as possible, moving through a dozen countries. We used weekends and what by American standards was a luxurious amount of vacation time to see as much as we could. After more than a decade in New York, we decided we were ready to see – to be – somewhere else. I remember hearing that Americans, a nation of wanderers, move more often than people in other countries, and it felt time that we do our part to uphold the transitory tradition.

III.

Over the course of a few weeks, piles of cardboard boxes grew around our apartment. We numbered each box with a black Sharpie and kept an inventory so we would be able to unpack efficiently. If we wanted to know where we had stowed the wall clock, bathroom garbage can, hair dryer, refrigerator magnets, battery-powered lantern, bike lock and chain, blank-page books and power strips, we would be ready (and when the box that actually did have such contents – number forty-one – and the others arrived, we were). When we taped shut the last carton, the total had reached 110.

The 110 boxes did not hold everything. A couple weeks before our September 11 departure (but after the one with the knife), we took a path-clearing trip to Portland. We rented a car and went shopping. Having the new place stocked with cooking oil and canned goods, batteries and cleaning supplies, a mop and a broom, a new vacuum cleaner and toilet paper would mean not having to go get all those elemental things while also trying to unpack and set up. It would be nice, we knew, to arrive and already have some meat in the freezer and cold beer in the refrigerator. We also got mundane dealings with banks and insurance companies out of the way. We made sure we had food and litter for the cats. Before leaving Brooklyn, we selected several things we did not want to entrust to the movers. These were not items of exceptional monetary value. We took our desert-island favorites: music, movies and books. Even if everything else we owned got lost or destroyed, we would still have sustaining listening, watching and reading. All of that, along with a coffee pot, a laptop computer and the clothes we also left on that preliminary expedition, would have filled a couple more boxes if they had not gone in suitcases. We sent things we wanted to receive sooner (another computer, a bicycle) separately by a faster method after we were told that our 110 boxes (as well as the furniture) could take more than a week to get to Oregon.

Another moving company estimate also affected what was ultimately delivered or, more accurately, what was not. Nancy and I had never thought of ourselves as thing-people. Our aesthetic favored the utilitarian over the decorative; we did not clutter our places with knickknacks, framed snapshots or other unnecessary dust-catchers. Besides, while Brooklyn's apartments may boast more square footage per dollar than Manhattan's, many of them still do not include much storage space. We had friends who did not have even a single closet. Such living quarters discourage hoarding. Or so I thought. As devoted readers, we had walls lined with bookcases. We did have closets, including one large enough for a file cabinet filled with old bank statements, bills and canceled checks. Our shredder broke before we could destroy all our unneeded documents filled with personal information.

We had another, more reliable method of dispensing of other, less private inessentials: the stoop sales that were part of culture in the neighborhood where we lived. On clear days in spring, summer and fall, residents would put books and baby clothes, furniture and toys, pans and pots, shoes and picture frames out on the steps and sidewalks in front of their brownstones and sell them. Frequently, as morning turned to afternoon and the quantity and appeal of used items diminished, sellers would become givers. They would leave what they did not want to take back inside their homes for passersby to pick up and haul into theirs. When we decided to go, we had to purge.

Relocating concentrates the mind on how people never stop paying for what they own. The simple transaction related to purchasing an item is the beginning of spending, not the end. After that, we pay to shelter or store what we bought. A key consideration in picking a place to live is whether it has room not only for people but also for their stuff. All those bookcases demand a room of their own. Insurance adds still more costs. When it comes time to take what has been acquired from one place to another, purported owners confront decisions about how much they are willing to continuing paying for their things. Even after selling what we deemed unworthy of taking across the country, and pitching what we should never have held onto in the first place, movers quoted prices that made us reconsider yet again what we thought we really wanted or needed. All those unused glasses might once have seemed worth keeping for large parties we never threw but now they revealed themselves to be unnecessary extravagances. Certain pieces of furniture and electrical appliances fit that classification too. Closets, it turns out, too easily hold clothes that don't fit or are never worn. So we held a second, even larger stoop sale.

While we had sold or given away books before, it never had been easy to part with them – until we learned what it would cost to keep them. Movers set their fees by weight, and book collections are heavy. Instantly those anthologies held onto since college became undeserving of the ongoing rent paid to keep housing them. The title story in *Unaccustomed Earth* involves a father who declines to share the large house in the Pacific Northwest where his daughter and husband moved from Park Slope, Brooklyn (the very same neighborhood Nancy and I were leaving). He prefers to remain in his small condominium because he likes the freedom from "all the things he'd recently gotten rid of, all the books and papers and clothes and objects one felt compelled to possess, to save." We did not entirely free ourselves of years' of accumulated things, but we did shed a good amount. In preparing for that second sale, we aggressively sought more and more to jettison. When we first started the reduction process, I worried that we might rashly dispose of things we would later wish we still had. I got over that. Breaking the compulsion to possess felt liberating. No one whose belongings exceed what fits in 110 boxes can claim to have slipped the shackles of materialism, but I know that the figure would have been much more absurdly large had we not gotten a sense of the freedom enjoyed by Lahiri's character.

IV.

Our earlier episodes of rootlessness did not present the same challenges that our escape from New York did. Alternating between campgrounds and cheap motels during an aimless cross-country ramble is easy when you are between semesters in graduate school or have a job you would happily quit. Abandoning a menial editing job for one paying a salary four times larger (and tax free) in the middle of Europe is easy too. Then, we did not own anywhere near enough to fill 110 boxes. We fit all we wanted into a few suitcases. We lived in furnished apartments. Abruptly changing course in middle age, especially with no new source of income, takes a greater effort of will.

For all the practical considerations surrounding the move – when to go, what to take – a major concern for me had been the wisdom of going at all. I knew that I wanted something else, a new set of experiences, another way of living, an unfamiliar landscape – unaccustomed earth! – but I also wrestled with an unexpected reluctance. The state of the economy worried voters more than, say, the war in Iraq or any other single issue at the time of the election, according to polls cited in news reports. Was this the time to make a change? Were we being imprudent? When I hesitated to commit to the plan – and I did hesitate – was I simply succumbing to fear?

Paradoxically, perhaps, recognizing that I felt scared made deciding what to do much easier. To stay put would mean living with the shame of submitting to a familiar but unsatisfying routine because of an ignoble unwillingness to hazard anything to break out of it. So what if, as I feared, the next place proved only different and not obviously better (as did turn out to be the case)? Different was the point, and different was good enough. Perhaps flinging ourselves across country did not make sense financially – another possible reason for caution. Or inaction. Did I really want *that* to determine how I lived? We went somewhere new this time because we chose to rather than out of economic necessity or because an unforeseen opportunity arose. The move could be tightly choreographed, but the reason for making it did not need to be straightforwardly sensible. Once I realized that the best reason to replant ourselves was because we wanted to and could, we did.

V.

Although the events of September 11, 2001, did not drive us out of New York, they did affect how we lived there for seven years afterwards. Catastrophes cause demands for action. The appearance of a concerted response must satisfy some human need even if it does not actually solve the catalyzing problems. When covering the 1968 Republican convention in Miami, Norman Mailer notices "echoes" of the then-recent assassination of Robert Kennedy in showy measures that provide no actual protection for candidates. When Nelson Rockefeller's airplane arrives, helicopters circle the airport as heavily armed police patrol on the ground. Yet Mailer never needed to show any identification to guards. He realizes that a would-be killer pretending to be a journalist could have easily carried a gun within a few feet of New York's governor. Such an assassin never would have gotten away, Mailer concedes, but he still could have hit his target, since the forces arrayed offer "no real security, just powers of retaliation." Forty years later, some things had changed, but much had not. After September 11, going anywhere without photo ID became much harder, but weaknesses in pretenses of security persisted. The echoes of September 11 involved police periodically standing at tables next to subway turnstiles and occasionally stopping passengers to look in their bags. Machine gun-equipped troops were widely deployed, and helicopters endlessly circled above, and not only at airports or when politicians moved through town. Yet if murderers plan on *not* escaping with their lives, then such armed pageants have no deterrent effect. Retaliatory powers do not matter to terrorists eager to obliterate themselves along with their victims. If a bomber willing to kill himself and numerous strangers failed to board the subway but were instead to self-detonate at a checkpoint, decimating multiple police officers as well as commuters, then his fellow fanatics would probably consider the act a success.

Even if I did not worriedly look at the gap in the skyline while traveling into or out of Manhattan, I knew while riding in crowded trains that if terrorists wanted to explode themselves and others during rush hour, they could. I never developed the New Yorker's capacity to pretend unpleasant realities did not exist or that other people's actions did not affect me. The random search charade provides nothing more than the illusion of greater safety. Security measures unlikely to do any more than give a modicum of comfort to those who feel that the authorities must "do something" became a part of every New Yorker's routine.

VI.

One thing many people deemed it necessary to do each September 11 after 2001 was to stage memorial events, like those presidential candidates attended the year we left New York. Not surprisingly, as inevitably happens with holidays, quasi-holidays and civil ceremonies, controversy over the content, and specifically the religious content, ensued. Even though religion motivated the followers of Osama bin Laden who flew jetliners into the World Trade Center, other zealots of the I-know-the-Truth-and-you're-doomed-if-you-don't-see-things-the-way-I-do type squealed with outrage when New York City's mayor, Michael Bloomberg, opted not to include preachers or other formal representatives of particular religious groups on the 2011 program. Bloomberg cited the perfectly reasonable and indisputable reality of too many religions existing in the city to be included. But those who complained weren't concerned about equal time for all faiths; they wanted a platform to espouse their own particular one. Reverend Pat Robertson, to cite one of the offended, said: "I am frankly shocked that Mayor Bloomberg thinks that he is doing the city of New York a favor by eliminating the spiritual element at an event commemorating tragedy, grief, and heroic sacrifice." Now I'm just guessing here, but I suspect that Robertson, who in *The New World Order* (1991) wrote of a Jewish-financed conspiracy for global domination, wasn't worried about the exclusion of rabbis from the day's doings. Anne Graham Lotz, the daughter of Reverend Billy Graham and author of books with titles like *Expecting to See Jesus* and *Heaven: My Father's House,* had this to say: "I've been convinced that 9/11 was our wakeup call. If that wouldn't wake up the church, what would it take?"

I never expected what happened on September 11 to function as a "wakeup call" to prompt widespread recognition that religious faith – and I mean religious faith in general and not loyalty to one specific brand of it – is not necessarily a positive quality and doesn't always bring out the best in people. I knew better than that. Even if that had happened, I as a humanist wouldn't have taken it as meaning the killings ultimately weren't so terrible after all, as another god-bothered Bloomberg critic implied was the case because the child of one victim went on to become a priest. (The most committed believers consistently appear to me as the best advertisements for nonbelief, but many people still buy the Bible babble they're selling.) Still, I did briefly wonder if belief would at least lose some of its status as an unquestioned virtue. After all, if September 11 didn't make people see faith's dangers, what would it take? Research by the Pew Forum on Religion and Public Life showed increases in the percentage of the U.S. population that doesn't subscribe to any religion – from 15 percent in 2007 to 20 percent in 2012 – but it's impossible to prove whether September 11 had anything to do with the change. (And four-fifths of the population still continued to believe.) Even though Bloomberg left religious professionals off the stage, the service conducted on it was not exclusively secular, including as it did several silent moments for prayer. He made a practical move; he intended no criticism.

Neither Robertson's nor Lotz's books were among those we took to Portland.

VII.

As we adapted to the new age, Nancy and I also started documenting our lives more carefully, considering them more closely and reflecting on them more intently. George Orwell, whose nonfiction I carried by hand to our new home out west, was a list-maker. He said he had "the sort of mind that takes pleasure in dates, lists, catalogues, concrete details, descriptions of processes, junk-shop windows, and back numbers" of old magazines. As our precise accounting of all we owned attests, Nancy and I both have that kind of mind too. Like Orwell, we started writing down every book we read each year. Trying to reassemble 2001's reading proved challenging. After several weeks or months go by, recalling precisely when a book was read can become difficult. In subsequent years we updated our individual bibliographies whenever we had a new book to add, noting the month when we finished each one. One of Orwell's biographers called the compilation of lists "a strange kind of addiction," and it can indeed be habit-forming. Eventually, we started keeping other lists: compact discs purchased, movies seen (in theaters on one list, at home on another), restaurants dined in and shows seen. While others attended the same events, dined where we enjoyed meals (or didn't), heard the same people talk, read the same books, heard the same recordings and watched the same movies (somewhere), our particular arrangement of experiences comprises our private histories. Lists like ours assist the memory, permitting their makers to recall experiences they otherwise might have forgotten. They also provide ways to assess states of existence by documenting how the list-keepers spent their time.

In Europe I would have called my passport my most valued possession because of where it made it possible for me to go. Later the volume Nancy and I refer to simply as The Book subsequently got that designation for preserving where we have been and what we have done amid our serial deracinations. The blue-spined journal with sewn-in ribbon bookmark filled with lists did not get packed in any of the 110 boxes. It came with us on a plane to a fresh patch of unaccustomed earth.

TWELFTH INTERLUDE

It warrants reiterating: place makes all the difference. Would I have the same ideas about Labor Day if I had grown up somewhere other than Detroit? Would I have the same perspective on my country if I hadn't lived in another? Would I carry with me the same thoughts and feelings about September 11, 2001, if I had been somewhere other than New York City that day?

Of course not.

Yet giving in to wanderlust doesn't necessarily mean fully severing roots or, more precisely, forgetting where one started. Someone temperamentally always looking forward to the next plot of unfamiliar territory may still find it necessary to return, mentally at least, to where he has already been.

Back to Detroit...

DETROIT UNDEAD

"What did they think they were celebrating?" Roger Micheldene wonders as his taxi passes "houses festooned with multi-coloured lights and orange-coloured turnip ghosts." Although I might ask the same question of many other holidays celebrated in the United States, I never shared the incomprehension of Halloween that Kingsley Amis's title character feels in *One Fat Englishman*. My father's elaborate Halloween displays might not have solved the mystery for Micheldene, if he could have seen them, but they made the point of the festivities clear to me. Indeed, his witches and zombies (without a turnip ghost, whatever that is, among them) made peculiar but perfect sense when and where he created them.

During the 1970s and 1980s in Detroit, the night before Halloween – Devil's Night – meant arson. Everything from the contents of garbage dumpsters to vacant buildings predictably went up in flames. People living next to empty houses – a common situation (then and later) – would stay home with garden hoses at the ready, intent on preserving their property amid the surrounding tinder. (I imagine Amis's disdainful protagonist would regard such orgies of deliberate destruction as typically American.) Only when I left the city to attend college in a place where buildings with "demolished by neglect" stenciled across their faded fronts were not common sights did I discover that what I thought was standard practice did not occur around the country each October 30. Once I politely explained that when I said I was from Detroit I did indeed mean the city and not one of its more affluent and less feared suburbs as fellow students frequently assumed, those from other places were as surprised to learn about Devil's Night there as I was to realize that setting fires was not how people elsewhere chose to celebrate.

Halloween in my hometown was another story. Despite the fiendish imagery, it offered positive relief after the smoke cleared. My memories of traipsing about the neighborhood – with parents when very small, with friends when slightly older but still young enough to spend hours gathering candy from neighbors – accorded pretty well with those of non-Detroiters. If Halloween itself had a sinister side then it took the form of widely circulating rumors of poisoned candy or razor blades embedded in apples. Cautious parents inspected wrappers for signs of tampering, but I don't remember any of them every finding suspicious sweets. (Fruit never made it to the inspection stage, at least among my discriminating circle of little sugar junkies, since we left it in the bushes wherever neighbors substituted such nutritious tricks for true treats.) Actually occurring seasonal catastrophes, from kids' perspectives, amounted to no more than cold temperatures requiring costume-covering winter coats. Though Halloween, like so many other holidays, may be haunted by pretend supernatural beings, no one really treats these specters, angels and demons as really existing or encourages others to do so. (Well, some Christians and Muslims do take seriously what they perceive as Halloween's devilish or occult imagery and point disapprovingly to its origins in the ancient Celtic harvest festival Samhain, but they haven't dissuaded many celebrants.) It's about imagination and play-acting, not faith and belief. Children express their fears, hopes and desires by temporarily transforming themselves into what scares them or inspires them or fascinates them at that brief, uninhibited moment before mundane adult concerns curdle innocent wishes into frustration and disappointment.

Trick-or-treaters are more than "ragged groups of people or children ... cavorting about," as Amis's overweight Brit dismisses them, and Halloween is not just for kids. Around the time I learned of other areas' fire-resistant autumns, my father began nurturing an enthusiasm for Halloween. One night a year, this usually not very demonstrative man would simultaneously don and doff a mask and gleefully provoke the squeals of happy fright that only children can make. When I was still young enough for trick-or-treating, my family's decorations consisted of the usual carved pumpkins, which would be placed inside the living room windows (and never on the front porch, where they'd likely have been smashed). Later on, my father added many other ornaments to his perennial winking jack-o'-lantern. He stationed an ax-wielding, gray-skulled giant with glowing red eyes near the stairs leading to the front door. Nearby a cape-wearing witch in red wool socks would hover on a broom. On one side of the turret, a large, fuzzy spider lurked noiselessly and patiently in a web; on the other side, a black cage held a skeleton that would, as my father twisted a knob on a repurposed train-set transformer, stand up to startle approaching confectionary seekers. Among the crooked, white, wooden crosses on the front lawn, Franken-stein's monster would sit up at similarly selected moments.

Situating the man-made man in a casket, as my father did, might not jibe with Mary Shelley's story of the new Pro-metheus, but the act of sparking animation in an assemblage of cast off bits and pieces evokes something of a place end-lessly struggling to resuscitate and rebuild itself. Called a dead or dying city when my parents moved there, at a time when other families of the same complexion were leaving, Detroit subsequently coagulated into a municipal *memento mori* as the industry that once attracted so many workers died and more and more people (including, temporarily, me) departed.

My father commenced building ghouls in his basement workshop at a moment when fewer and fewer children walked door to door collecting candy from their neighbors. Instead, parents drove their small ghosts, princesses, athletes, celeb-rities and superheroes to certain parts of the city, carefully selecting where to let them solicit sweets. The kids who re-mained close to home stopped ringing every doorbell like their predecessors used to do; instead, they only went to the houses where people they knew and trusted lived. Neverthe-less, on Halloween several hundred children still stopped by my parents' place. It became something of an institution, a miniature tradition of its own. Individuals who years earlier went there for a treat would return years later to accompany the next generation among my father's home-made monsters even though they did not live in the neighborhood, or in the city, anymore.

Around the same time my father formed his army of the undead, the Renaissance City, as Detroit in an episode of desperate optimism dubbed itself, starting having some success squelching Devil's Night. If my father set out to revive anything with his holiday activities, it was not so much the city as his own imagination. While having a mechanical creature arise from a coffin might suggest resurrection and renewal, the black box also conveniently concealed the jury-rigged system of weights and gears that perform the work of lifting the monster's visible torso and head. Because of these things my father fabricated, mostly from found objects, Halloween for me is synonymous with the pleasure of creativity. The witch, the spider, the Frankenstein's monster and the other figures first arrived when he began seriously pursuing another, year-round artistic endeavor, one closely aligned with both his Halloween devices and the city where he created them. Near the end of a career as a computer systems engineer he immersed himself in photography. After accepting an offer to retire early and closeting the costume of white shirt and business suit, he intently, even passionately, pursued image-making. He joined a photography club and collected more awards than he knew what to do with. While taking the sorts of pictures of lighthouses, wooden bridges, waterfalls and flowers that appeal to tourists visiting the northern Michigan galleries that agreed to sell his work, he did not confine himself to any single style or subject matter. He also started exploring dilapidated buildings – Detroit's once-grand train station, stalled former car factories, shuttered schools, those empty houses and burned-out buildings – and chronicling shattered scenes of urban decay.

In what had been a darkroom until digital cameras displaced film and it became a place to store his work, he hung a small picture of the precise point where his various interests intersect: a photograph of a house in Detroit in full-fledged Halloween mode. His visual imagination yields two- and three-dimensional results, but the motivation behind both remains the same. In addition to composing scenes of blossoming nature and of a collapsing city, he developed something of a specialty in staged shots of things. Using the same skills he applied to materializing monsters, he produced pictures like the one purporting to have captured a baseball just as it crashes through a window or a strawberry on a spoon presumably held by an out-of-frame hand. (The latter became one of his top-sellers, and he does like generating crowd-pleasers.) My father would play around with methods for manipulating pictures (many of which predate the digital era) and insert a moon in a sky where there hadn't been one, place a person in what had been an empty window or add a few extra yellow cabs into an only partially congested street. Still, I think he formed a real fondness for the photographs that involved skills not only with a camera and a computer but also with a hammer and wire cutters. These creations permitted him to indulge most fully his too-long-deferred impulses to make things for people to see – and to do so in a disintegrating metropolis where they, like an Amis character, don't expect to find anything worth admiring.

THIRTEENTH INTERLUDE

It becomes necessary to go to the root. Time and place – history, that is – are what we're dealing with. In "Jack Johnson's Fourth of July" I stress that when events occur contributes crucially to their significance. Even if tradition upholders forget or overlook what gave rise to their customs, those buried origins and intentions can still have a force in the present. Do what you do, but know why you're doing it, I say (and Father P. could have written on a sign). This requires looking far back before one's own personal experiences of holidays like Thanksgiving, which intersects historically with a different kind of fighting than Johnson's.

NO THANKS

As its prayerful name announces, Thanksgiving Day involves the bending of knees. To whom, after all, would celebrants give thanks if not to "Him"? In what became the United States, residents of Plymouth in the Massachusetts colony headed by Governor William Bradford initiated the tradition in 1621, at least according to the conventional account. Historians have questioned whether Plymouth really was the site of the first Thanksgiving, whether the date is accurate, and whether early colonial events were not more akin to carnivals with feasts than holy days with formal services. Regardless of when, where or how they did so, the grateful didn't thank goodness or luck; they thanked God.

The date for collectively acting on this religious impulse remained unsettled for the next couple of centuries. All the colonies gave thanks simultaneously for the first time during the Revolutionary War in October 1776. Congress designated December 18 as the day for doing so the following year. Thanksgiving Days occurred on various dates of state governors' choosing until the Civil War, when Abraham Lincoln decided a president "had as good a right to thank God as a Governor." His October 3, 1863, Thanksgiving Day Proclamation, which transformed what had been a patchwork of regional festivals held at different times of year into a uniform national holiday, explicitly invokes devotion to a deity by calling on citizens "in every part of the United States, and also those who are at sea and those who are sojourning in foreign lands, to set apart and observe the last Thursday of November next as a day of thanksgiving and praise to our beneficent Father who dwelleth in the heavens."

American Thanksgiving Day from the start also mixed

worldly stuff with its sacred ingredients. Unlike holidays with scriptural bases, such as Easter, it relies on mythical tales about the founding and development of the United States, schoolhouse stories of pilgrims appreciatively receiving the blessing God bestowed on their colonial project and, implicitly at least, on the nation that grew out of it. The popular imagery involving black-clad, log cabin-dwelling pilgrims with buckles on their shoes sitting down to a meal with corn on the cob and cranberries – none of that has any historical basis. Pilgrims and Puritans – which are not the same things – may have both migrated to America for religious reasons, but whether they ate turkey on the first Thanksgiving, wherever and whenever that took place, remains unknown. Indeed, days of thanksgiving actually predated the trip across the ocean from England to what became Massachusetts. In the 1500s, Puritans, opposed to the numerous Catholic holidays cluttering the calendar, including Easter and Christmas, initiated the practice of instead holding days of thanksgiving in response to what they perceived as special blessings from God. The first American Thanksgiving of legend probably was one of these days, held because of a good harvest.

Thanks-givers may have always acknowledged what Lincoln calls "the everwatchful providence of almighty God," but they did so for specific incidents of beneficence received – or desperately sought. "Through all stages of historic development feasts were linked to moments of crisis, of breaking points in the cycle of nature or in the life of society or man," literary philosopher Mikhail Bakhtin writes in *Rabelais and His World* (1965). "Moments of death and revival, of change and renewal always led to a festive perception of the world." Plymouth colonists may have started the ritual routine (perhaps in the summer of 1623) because a lengthy drought finally ended. Nearly two and half centuries later, the president recruited God to the side of the Union forces in the Civil War. Lincoln commended to His care "all those who have become widows, orphans, mourners or sufferers in the lamentable civil strife in which we are unavoidably engaged." He also "fervently implore[d] the interposition of the almighty hand to heal the wounds of the nation, and to restore it, as soon as may be consistent with Divine purposes, to the full enjoyment of peace, harmony, tranquility, and union." He repeated these same sentiments in his second inaugural address, as historian Doris Kearns Goodwin notes in *Team of Rivals* (2005). Lincoln may not have been the most devout of presidents. As an adult he never joined a congregation. His former law partner, William Herndon, called him a rationalist with no taste for the supernatural and doubts about the immortality of the soul. Nonetheless, the document he signed says what it says (and that second inaugural address does contain many biblical references, reflecting either a late-in-life turn to sincere religiosity or politically calculated hypocrisy).

Of course, for many Thanksgiving proponents, the day isn't about politics or providence; it's about poultry. It is a feast, after all. In *Pudd'nhead Wilson* (1894), Mark Twain writes of Thanksgiving Day: "Let all give humble, hearty, and sincere thanks, now, but the turkeys." While this lacks Twain's usual incisive wit, it implies that just a few decades after Lincoln set the date, Americans thought mainly about the meal. "Gratitude and treachery are merely the two extremities of the same procession," Twain writes in the same novel. "You have seen all of it that is worth staying for when the band and the gaudy officials have gone by." Hungry Revolutionary Warriors might have noticed the same connection. On the eve of their march to Valley Forge to set up winter quarters, George Washington's ill-provisioned troops wondered why they should feel thankful as directed. One soldier wrote in his diary: "this being the third day we have been without flour or bread – & are living on a high uncultivated hill, in huts & tents lying on the cold ground, upon the whole I think all we have to be thankful for is that we are alive & not in the grave." In a late story, "Hunting the Deceitful Turkey" (1906), Twain says the fowl is born both with a bone that makes a perfect hunter's bird-call and a talent for tricking pursuers and getting itself out of trouble. As an emblem of "Nature's treacheries," it's a suitable dish for Thanksgiving Day, when some enjoy a grand feast while others get only a taunting reminder of want.

The war to establish rather than preserve the nation gave rise not only to famished Thanksgiving Day questioners; it also initiated a different holiday of appreciation, albeit a local one. "For more than a century," biographer Ron Chernow says in *Alexander Hamilton* (2004), "November 25, 1783, was commemorated in New York City as Evacuation Day, the blessed end to seven years of British rule and martial law." Of course, there had been more than seven years of British rule if one considers the years prior to the Revolutionary War, but in September 1776 the British army made its headquarters in New York. During the occupation, the city was ravaged by a massive fire and thousands of revolutionary soldiers and supporters were held in prison ships. So the conflict's conclusion ("blessed" or otherwise) and the departure of redcoats warranted special notice there. According to a *Harpers New Monthly Magazine* article on Evacuation Day's centenary, on the actual day in 1783, American soldiers tried to raise the Stars and Stripes after the Union Jack had been taken down at Fort George in lower Manhattan only to find that the British had taken the rope and tackle along with their flag and had also greased the flagpole. Undeterred, a resourceful young soldier equipped himself with cleats and nails and managed to work his way up the pole, install new halyards and raise the flag. The image of that event came to symbolize the day and its resonant secular significance: a successful fight for liberty.

Before the more spiritual holiday displaced it from the calendar, no-nonsense Evacuation Day marked change and renewal – the death of one type of society and the birth of a new one – with a refreshing freedom from theological overtones. It suggested the realization of just the sort of republic envisioned by Thomas Paine, who contributed to both the U.S. and the French Revolutions: one subservient to neither gods nor kings. At the 1883 centennial celebration, New York Mayor Franklin Edson, confident of the holiday's sustaining resonance, said it should be honored by all people who "found upon these shores a refuge from exactions and acts of oppression by ruler of foreign countries."

During the decade I lived in the city, I mentioned Evacuation Day to acquaintances, including many lifelong New Yorkers, and not one had ever even heard of it. Possible explanations for Evacuation Day's demise immediately present themselves. Perhaps the very specificity of the defunct day's reason for being – troops leaving the city – undermined its ability to endure. Even though Lincoln in 1863 envisioned Thanksgiving Day on the day he selected as a one-time, morale-boosting, war-time event, it ended up recurring annually on the last Thursday of November because the holiday's broadness – its call to reflect on whatever one might feel grateful for – allowed it to adapt and persist. With the Fourth of July recognized as the annual celebration of independence, Evacuation Day could be considered redundant. When, during World War I, the United States and Britain joined forces as allies, cheering the long-in-the-past end of British occupation came to seem unseemly, if not irrelevant. However, if banks and other businesses can close for days connected with both the birth and the death of one religion's messiah, then I see nothing wrong with holidays marking both the start and the end of the Revolutionary War. (One of the better aphorisms from Pudd'nhead Wilson's calendar concerns Independence Day: "Statistics show that we lose more fools on this day than in all the other days of the year put together. This proves, by the number left in stock, that one Fourth of July per year is now inadequate, the country has grown so.") Besides, glorifying the end of hostilities, rather than their commencement, gave Evacuation Day an especially upbeat tone.

Still, the war angle, I suspect, could be an issue for some. The forgotten regional November holiday ties directly to the fighting that formally concluded in the interval between the

Declaration of Independence and the Constitution. The undiminished national holiday connects meaningfully to the Civil War, but this bit of history, apparently, can easily be ignored.

Indeed, most Americans do overlook it. After all, Thanksgiving is popularly associated with events that predate the War Between the States. Secessionists and unionists just do not factor into it. Instead, it's about pilgrims fleeing religious persecution and friendly Indians welcoming them to a new land and sharing its bounty. Unless it's about imperialism and genocide. Differences of opinion exist on that score. If you put forth the interpretation less amenable to children's pageants involving elaborate, old-fashioned headwear, the one that touches on the dishonorable treatment of the native population that lived in what became the United States, then you are likely to be dismissed as some sort of crank, or so I have found.

Focusing on Thanksgiving Day's religiosity – either to endorse it or to explain an aversion to the holiday – can also raise eyebrows among the go-with-the-flow set. In an essay about "religiously minded supporters of Thanksgiving" and their efforts to amplify the day's spirituality, Andrew Santella wonders: "Do we really have to choose between the extremes of calling Thanksgiving a religious holiday or a civic celebration, a day more like Easter or more like the Fourth of July? Or can't we assume that the holiday has evolved as some more subtle mix of the secular and the spiritual, one that each of us can adjust according to our own values?" This sort of it-means-whatever-I-want-it-to-mean attitude might accord with most Americans' actual observations of Thanksgiving (and some other holidays), but it doesn't sit well with me. If, as Santella writes in *Slate,* "expressing gratitude for the good things in life is in some sense an inherently spiritual act," then Thanksgiving is in a very definite sense a religious holiday.

As someone who sees no evidence of Lincoln's "most high God, who while dealing with us in anger for our sins, hath nevertheless remembered mercy" or the divine plan that permits both "fruitful fields" and "the waste that has been made in the camp, the siege, and the battlefield," I have no use for a government-sanctioned call to devotion. Memorializing vanquished soldiers' departure from a land that revolted against monarchy and started down the road to democracy appeals to me in a way that thanking "our beneficent Father," whether for a bountiful harvest or for presumed intervention in military campaigns, does not. Something in me rebels against observing religious holidays, even diluted, indeterminate, supposedly "evolved" ones. Instead of thanking God (or even "goodness," as some euphemistically call him), I prefer celebrating independence. This, I hasten to add, can be done at Evacuation Day feasts featuring turkeys, Benjamin Franklin's preferred choice for the national bird.

FOURTEENTH INTERLUDE

It is not necessary to uncover the next holiday's unacknowledged religious association. There is none. What Christmas is all about is plain to see. Yet many of the strands weaving through this volume intertwine during this birthday party. Childhood memories, travel, commerce, seasonal changes, friends, family, literature, music, death and hideous decorations – it's got it all. If there's one day on which blind conformity and considered living battle it out, this is it.

No matter how much I might like to, I can't skip Christmas entirely ...

CHRISTMAS THINGS

You don't want to miss this. That's what I was told.

Having believed since childhood that the couple living across the street from my parents – or the man, at least – disliked me, I never expected to be invited over for a Christmas drink. Initially I'd been reluctant to go, but my parents, who'd started socializing with the couple while I'd been away at college and had seen the inside of their place, said it was not an invitation to turn down. I'd been in the house before, but not since the elderly couple occupied it. A family with children around my age had lived there when I was quite young, but they'd moved out many years earlier, and the pair, who seemed old even then, became a presence for much of my childhood.

They were hard not to notice. They always owned several large Cadillacs, huge 1960s and 1970s models, which they would frequently rearrange in the driveway, backing out the red convertible and the dark blue limousine so the big black two-door would be ready to go the next day. They never put any of them in their two-car garage. She never said much to me or the other neighborhood children. Instead, the silent, cigarette-smoking woman in slippers and a terrycloth robe would drag a German shepherd with nonfunctioning hind legs around their expansive lawn. Their yard was bigger than most in the neighborhood, consisting of what could have been two lots. The previous tenants had used the extra outdoor space during at least one winter to make a simple ice-skating rink for the kids. They even had a jungle gym out back. Children played in that area no more, however. The old man, a high school principal, was the type who would bark if a ball or a child's foot touched his property. Perhaps a lifetime among school children can make a man into someone who, when

- 153 -

at home, simply craves peace and freedom from kid sounds. Only later, when I had sufficiently outgrown offending youthfulness, did I discover how far they went to create a sanctuary for themselves.

The couple did not just collect large automobiles. They did not merely collect this or that. They collected as if the verb were intransitive: they collected. Two people managed to make a house with four bedrooms on the second floor and a few more on the third as well as a basement feel cramped. They filled all that space with lacquered little boxes, gilded birdcages, candlesticks, clocks, chairs, vases and tchotchkes of all sizes and shapes. Pictures, mirrors, plates, sconces, tapestries and paintings covered the walls so that hardly any painted plaster could be seen. When someone wondered aloud how they kept the place clean, the couple explained that they would go one room at a time and take however many days or weeks – weeks! – it took to wipe, polish and shine everything. They required about a year to go through each room in the house, and then they would repeat the cycle.

Anywhere there was room to put something, they put something. But the place wasn't a residence-turned-warehouse and they weren't the husband and wife equivalent of Homer and Langley Collyer, the notoriously compulsive New York City packrats. Items had been placed and arranged with care. They were not in storage; they were on display, even if in an idiosyncratic way. The couple used the built-in shelves in a room designed as a study not for books but for their collection of ceramic, pirate-head-shaped Toby mugs. They devoted a room upstairs to their numerous stuffed animals made by Steiff, a German outfit that claims to have invented the teddy bear. Some of these were small enough to hold in the palm of one's hand; another was large enough to fill the seat of an airplane, which is how they transported it back after acquiring it on one of their frequent European trips. (More stuffed animals hung as a plush, furry, lightless chandelier from a rack in the kitchen that other people would have used for pots and pans.) The couple knew someone involved in the Iranian hostage crisis of 1979 to 1981, and they dedicated another room to that event, decorating it with related framed photos and newspaper clippings, including a magazine cover with the Ayatollah Khomeini's image.

Amid the unusual excess of their home, the pair did uphold the standard holiday conventions. Even with all the furniture – the couches (one covered in what looked like zebra skin), the fleet of end tables, and the cabinets displaying the knickknacks that did not fit on the mantle place or the coffee tables – the couple found room to wedge two Christmas trees. One tree would not have been sufficient to hold their collection of ancient holiday ornaments. With so many objects arrayed over every horizontal surface it was hard to find a place to set down the tarnished silver tankard of unsettlingly lumpy homemade eggnog that had been handed to me when I first stepped on to the rugs overlapping each other on the floor.

My parents also habitually partook of many, but not all, Christmas day trappings. When I was still a child, long before I visited the hall of curiosities across the street, my family celebrated Christmas as though Jesus had nothing to do with it. I experienced it as time away from school and for the presents children love receiving. Every December, we would drive out to a farm where tree-hunters could tromp through snow and ride in a hay-filled, tractor-pulled wagon prior to sawing down a conifer, which would then be strapped to the top of the car, taken home and propped up next to the living room windows. My mother would thread together popcorn and cranberries to wind around it. We exchanged gifts. We saw relatives typically seen no other time of year, unless at other major holidays. Though my mother would play classical Christmas music on the stereo, there were no trips to church. There were no prayers. My tall father would reach up and place a papier-mâché dove, not a star or an angel, on top of the tree.

Indeed, until a Jesuit education abruptly ended my pleasantly Christ-free existence, Jesus played no part, at any time of year, in my childhood, at least not in the way he must have for his adherents. I never stopped believing in that or any other god because I'd never started. Churchgoing simply was not how we spent Sundays. My parents did attend a Unitarian church for a while, or so I've been told. (I was quite young when they gave that up and I retain no memories of it.) They not only convinced themselves that Christmas could be observed free of its inherent religiosity; they also believed that they could send me to Catholic school simply because it offered a better education than the public school in our area, as if the religious component were somehow separable from the others.

In one way or another, however, religious education leaves its marks. Among the Jesuits, my attitude toward religion evolved from the ignorance and indifference of early childhood to annoyance and rejection. Priests only, if inadvertently, confirmed that Jesus existed only in stories. Once I grasped that Christmas had something to do with this character, I wondered why my family went through the motions of celebrating Christmas at all. Jesus was not someone we knew, let alone loved, so what was all the fuss about?

Holidays satisfy some deep emotional need, or so one rationale goes, and the religious elements of days like Christmas are not the essential ones. Certainly many people claim to enjoy holidays' traditional forms and disregard their contents. Barbara Ehrenreich, author of *Dancing in the Streets: A History of Collective Joy* (2007), posits a "human imperative to celebrate." She claims that, in pre-modern times at least, "holidays bonded whole communities together, not just families." People like my parents who regard the God-part of Christmas as detachable perpetuate the conventions because they share Ehrenreich's longing for holidays as "occasions for communal joy." (Why, in the name of community togetherness, people travel great distances from where they live might count as a true Christmas mystery.)

Certainly, the appeal of getting together with friends and family, partaking of a feast, expressing affection for each other through the exchange of gifts is readily apparent. (And, yes, it may be powerful enough actually to account for widespread willingness to embark on long journeys in lousy winter weather.) For nonbelievers no less than the faithful, the shared bonds of human connections nourish existence. For me and at least some other secularists, however, treating holidays as à la carte menus from which celebrants can pick and choose – "I'll have the family dinner, hold the saying of grace, and then gifts, no prayers, thanks" – is ultimately unappetizing and unsatisfying. No matter how much secularly minded people might want to ignore it, religious holidays' religiousness never fully fades away. I can appreciate the motives of the pair of New Jersey Humanist Network members, Gary Brill and Joe Fox, who created HumanLight, as a nonreligious holiday set for December 23 and for which celebrants are encouraged to develop their own traditions. Yet the proximity to Christmas suggests that HumanLight simply reconfigures that à la carte approach of keeping the humanist-friendly bits and tossing the rest, including the original holiday's name. I tend to agree with Tom Flynn, author of *The Trouble with Christmas* (1992), who argues that atheists, humanists and freethinkers do themselves a disservice by celebrating Christmas or euphemistic alternatives like HumanLight or solstice. Rather than declining the invitation to observe a Christian holiday and treating Christmas as nothing special, they instead perpetuate at least some of its traditions and confer validity on a religious holiday by doing so.

I don't think I'm deficient in the urge to celebrate. I am no Malvolio denying others their cakes and ale and long weekends. At the same time, I do think the reasons for holiday observation matter. Those who take the Bible stories as revealed truth may be credulous, but at least they do what they do on December 25 out of sincerity. Non-believing clingers to familiar traditions, in contrast, resort to transparent sophistry for justification. Some argue that the Church imposed commemoration of Christ's birth on an existing pagan festival, which makes the holiday, if looked at in dim light from just the right angle, not Christian at all. Besides, so-called Christmas trees have no biblical basis, which makes them not religious, really; they're just symbols of life surviving through winter.

Those trees are put up because it's Christmas. Those who pretend otherwise are doing just that: pretending. Perhaps some people somewhere once did something similar for somewhat different reasons a couple of millennia ago, but the intervening history cannot be so easily disregarded. (Romans may have celebrated the birth of the god Mithra on December 25 until Constantine imposed Christianity on the empire, but impose it he did. Moreover, the pagan parties involved bread and wine representing the body and blood of a deity who descended to Hades and was resurrected after three days. So pointing approvingly to pagan sources hardly drains the day of religiosity.) Some of that history may involve certain Christians who believed the pagan-tinged holiday was insufficiently pure, but it's fair to say that most denominations came around to seeing it as the day to commemorate the birth of Jesus. I may not agree with Christian crusaders on much, but when groups like Focus on the Family and the Catholic League say Christmas is about Christ, I don't dispute it even if, unlike them, I see this as not as a reason to observe the holiday but as the reason not to. Although Christmas gift-givers might not consciously imitate three reputedly wise men, they still treat this particular time of year as something special, as at least some believers have done for centuries. Even quasi-secular celebrations retain the taint of the numinous.

As does another holiday originally devised as an alternative to Christmas. One of the seven core principles of Kwanza, which Maulana Ndabezitha Karenga, né Ronald McKinley Everett, launched as a distinct African American year-end holiday, is *imani*, or faith. Moreover, in time Kwanza became amenable to the participation of Christians and celebrators of Christmas. When the mother in Ntozake Shange's 1982 novel *Sassafrass, Cypress & Indigo* discovers that one of her daughters has dropped Christmas in favor of Kwanza, she initially believes she's failed as a parent. "Still," she then realizes, "as long as it's a religious ceremony with feasts and gifts like Christmas, I guess it'll be okay." Variants are palatable as long as those essentials are retained.

The parent-child dynamic Shange touches on is not a trivial one. In my pre-Jesuit-school youth, I enjoyed the Christmas-Eve anticipation and the Christmas-morning family gift exchange around the tree as much as any other child could have. It was only once I got the background information about the holiday that I decided I could do without it. As Flynn points out, those who dispense with religion often do so later on in life than I, who never had it anyway, did. Many former believers who contemplate canceling religious holiday observations once they shed their faith find it difficult to persuade their families to halt traditions like decorating Christmas trees and giving gifts. Indeed, my wife says she could have seen carrying on with Christmas Lite like many nonbelievers if we'd had children. Never having had to navigate these waters, I won't say just how I would have. I will point out that going along with what others do on a particular day even if you disagree with the fundamentally religious reasons for doing it might not be the best example to set for youngsters.

While Ehrenreich might be right about people's propensity to party, the communal component she extols can easily become coercive. For me, Christmas is no more meaningful than Hanukkah or Ramadan, but I've never been expected to celebrate those (at least not yet). If you don't belong to the community of the faithful, then almost-mandatory group celebrations based on religious beliefs aren't joyful. A pervasive, persistent assumption that everyone – unless he or she belongs to another popular confessional group, and perhaps even then – should carry on at least some traditions connected with Christmas makes itself felt toward the end of each year. Who doesn't like shiny lights twinkling everywhere (even if tax dollars were used to install some of the religiously-motivated decorations)? Only some sort of eccentric wouldn't want to give and receive gifts, right?

Although I know the collectors exchanged gifts among themselves – after he died, she found boxes of presents he'd purchased for her hidden away in a closet – I never learned what religious beliefs, if any, they held. They certainly were dedicated to tangible things, but then so are many true believers. The face of Pope John Paul II looked down from at least one plate on a crowded wall, but it might have offered evidence of nothing more than a visit to Rome. Souvenirs from Caesar's Palace hung nearby. At both of their funerals I heard the usual platitudes about an afterlife. Of course what is said during such rituals often has no meaningful connection to the people commemorated (even as the regular repetition of those ceremonial forms – whether at funerals or during holidays – lends the veneer of legitimacy to the religious ideas behind them). Their temple to materialism manifested year-round the acquisitiveness other Americans indulge most openly at Christmastime, but the couple may have regarded the season itself simply as merely one of the traditional times for people to get together. While they hosted Christmas gatherings, their holiday-related efforts seemed somewhat half-hearted. Yes, dual indoor trees' branches bore seasonal decorations – and there was that eggnog. But there were also the bushes outdoors, the big green ones in the front yard extending the width of the house, upon which the man would casually string a single, short strand of colored lights, as if to acknowledge the fact of the holiday, but only grudgingly, and in the most minimal possible way. This from a household dedicated to extreme decoration. While the man may not have been the ogre he seemed to small children, he remained something of a grouch, grumbling barbed comments about my parents' next door neighbors, the gay (and childless) antique dealers who were probably the couple's closest friends in the neighborhood. The Santa Claus hat covering his bald head did nod slightly toward a holiday spirit, though that may have been ironically intended.

After experiencing Christmas with the collectors, I did, reluctantly, attend a few tree-trimming parties where a more openly winking tone prevailed. My hosts shared the belief that holidays like Christmas could be primarily social affairs – excuses, as if any were needed, for friends to gather, eat and drink. Though not to the unsurpassable extent of the Cadillac drivers, these celebrants also prized the holiday's kitsch factor, expressing the aesthetic sensibility of Las Vegas – that neon caricature of American excess – in living rooms with flashing lights, brightly colored glass baubles, plastic trinkets and sparkly garlands. They did this not despite but because *tinsel* and *tacky* are synonymous. Here ornaments were more likely to be treasured for silliness than solemnity. If the older Christmas fellow travelers sought to insulate themselves from life's unpleasantness by surrounding themselves with stuff, the younger ones celebrated Christmas by flouting Saint Paul's example and refusing to put away childish things. If pressed, these peers might have acknowledged the regrettable forfeiture of the human capacity for reason represented by honoring the birth of a fictional messiah on a day when even those who swear he actually existed don't really believe he was born. Nevertheless, they submitted to exactly what aggravates me about holidays and religion: the willingness to do, in some form or another, what others have always done because of foundationless teachings that that is what we're all supposed to do. Even if Elvis Presley figurines and characters from the holiday television specials that members of my generation invariably watched replace angels and more traditional emblems, Christmas trees look to me like the abject capitulation to superstitious weak-mindedness.

Yes, I know the gospels present conflicting accounts of Jesus' birth and none of them says he arrived on December 25, but the holiday nonetheless exists as it does now to honor a character I don't recognize as divine. I also know the odds are against anything I say here persuading true believers to embrace reason and skepticism and to abandon the fairy tales that console them or supply them with easy answers to the hard questions. And I'm fully aware that many non-believers insist on Christmas trees' pre-Christian heritage and think such decorations can be divorced from religion. But I'm still not buying it: they're called Christmas trees and are put up on the day set aside to mark the birth of Christ. I recognize that some of my fellow secularists believe changing the name and (very slightly) the date solves the problems I have with Christmas things. For me at least, it doesn't.

The novelty of a skeptic at the Christmas party wears off for everyone. I decided not to carry on the role of the curmudgeon on the couch cracking wise about his friends. Instead, I chose to decline all invitations to a ghost's birthday party and to shun Christmas things as much as possible. I have no religious faith, I have no Christmas tree, and I want neither.

And I don't believe I've missed a thing.

LAST INTERLUDE

The ways people arrive at their beliefs matter no less than what they believe. As I've tried to drive home in these pages, inherited ideas – those held simply because they were passed down by others – don't necessarily have value in my estimation. Those ideas that hold up to close inspection after having been arrived at through independent thinking, now those deserve some respect. As far as I can tell, people who ask questions rather than accept what authority figures tell them, who require evidence rather than take things on faith, who tend more toward the ironic than the strictly literal, and who have a more cosmopolitan than parochial outlook, tend not to be religious types. They, in my experience, are more apt to believe – and demonstrate – that one can lead a moral and meaningful life without any religious faith. They conclude that the life they're living is the only one they'll ever live, so they might as well make the most of it.

Despite what some folks with religious convictions might conclude, people can indeed have a very rich experience as secularists. Appreciation of beauty demands no devotion to a deity. A sense of wonder requires no resort to the supernatural. We don't need to be commanded to love. Submission to an invented higher power can discourage rather than promote curiosity. Contemplation, reflection and introspection don't belong exclusively to spiritual practice. And vital traditions don't need to have any scriptural underpinning to bring people together.

All of which brings me back to those lists I discuss in "One Hundred and Ten Boxes." Nancy and I never made lists for lists' sake alone. We refer to them; we discuss them. We developed a New Year's Eve tradition of jointly reviewing our individual, annual books lists together, discussing which books we'd both read, which new authors we'd discovered, which books one of us thought the other might like. Our little family's end-of-year review in many years also included assessing the music we acquired.

As we come to the end of the wine opened at the start of this cycle of true stories, I offer the following account of this process to illustrate how one humanist's mind works when pondering an art form that elevates and sustains that part of the mind popularly called the soul.

YEAR-END TOP TEN

At the end of many years, I made lists of my ten favorite albums released in the preceding twelve months. Although this particular New Year's Eve tradition of artistic contemplation ceased to be an annual event when, for one reason or several, I didn't acquire enough disks to rank, I still think it was worth doing. Here's a list of the reasons why.

1. *Self-examination.* List-making requires introspection and reflection. Sure, it's also a simple way of keeping track of things, a method of organization. Those kinds of lists are useful, and I rely on them. I formed the habit of maintaining several annual lists – books read, movies seen and so on – and these reflect my judgment and taste to some extent. But the top-ten compact disk lists really required thought to assemble. Doing so involved closely considering personal preferences. Often an album's top-ten status is apparent upon first listen. An especially pleasant occurrence for a music lover is to hear new music and immediately think it's something to return to again and again, to suspect you're experiencing a happy part of your future. In magical years of wondrous musical bounty when more than ten of these entered my life, the list-making forced me to do some aesthetic exercise and critical culling. In years when for whatever reason I found only a few obvious top-tenners, I had to sort out what I liked best of the rest. Either way, making the lists told me something about myself – even if it was nothing more than that I sometimes lacked discretion and restraint in record stores.

2. *Mild mental calisthenics.* List-making requires setting parameters, and the rules also say something about the person who makes them. Compiling a list of well-liked releases from a given year might seem like a straightforward affair, but

complications inevitably arise. The Thelonious Monk Quartet with John Coltrane played Carnegie Hall in 1957 but the recording of their set went unissued for several decades. Could music made in the middle of the twentieth century be in top-ten contention in the twenty-first century? (I voted yes and put *At Carnegie Hall* on my 2005 list.) What about something like 2003's *The Complete Jack Johnson Sessions*? Though most of the music on the five-CD set had not been previously released, edited portions of it had appeared on *Jack Johnson* and *Big Fun,* two electrified Miles Davis albums from the 1970s. (Because parts of it had been commercially available, I left it off my list even though I instantly recognized the claim it staked to a sizeable territory of my mental landscape.) I guess this makes me firm but flexible – or fastidious and foolish. I tried to follow consistently what I realized were arbitrary guidelines. Arbitrariness characterized the entire endeavor. After all, at the end of each December I ignored the CDs first released more than 365 days before, which always outnumbered the current year's lot. Some items that probably would have made a list I didn't hear until the following year or later. Considering all the music absorbed, regardless of copyright date, might have allowed for a fuller assessment of a given sonic year, but that's not the approach I took. The niggling involved in determining what qualifies for inclusion on my top-ten lists helped keep my mind in shape for less trivial kinds of mental work, or so I'd like to think. In any case, list-making beats doing crossword puzzles.

3. *Critical workout.* List-making promotes rigorous critical thinking. Figuring out what qualifies for consideration is just the beginning. Fully engaged listening is not a passive activity. Often, deciding between a few potential top-ten designees meant careful track-by-track scrutiny. A single okay-but-not-exceptional song could be the undoing of an otherwise solid effort. If I weren't going to make a list, I might not have thought as much about each part of each album, and this critical listening entailed figuring out what qualities give mu-

sic the power to affect me. Identifying the work with the most vitality calls for the vigorous analysis that makes real appreciation and enjoyment possible.

4. Self-portraiture. Lists can become a kind of unadorned autobiography. A random grocery list reveals something about the shopper who made it – his preferences and appetites, perhaps her economic class and maybe even hints about ethnic or regional background. A list of what music most moved a person provides an even more intimate, personal picture – a snapshot of the soul. I'm not a professional music critic. Even when I purchased excessive numbers of CDs, I never obtained enough for my lists to say anything significant about the state of music. (Did trumpeter Dave Douglas really make some of the tastiest albums several years in a row, or did I just buy each consecutive addition to his catalogue?) Instead, they tell anyone who cares to look at them about a solitary man. To my way of thinking (which might only be shared by fanatics like those novelist Nick Hornby depicts in *High Fidelity*), the fact that the list with Monk and Coltrane on it also names guitar wizard Sonny Landreth and country titan George Jones (as well as Douglas) reveals something more essential about me than a stray reminder to get bread and laundry detergent ever could.

5. Growth chart. A series of annual top-ten lists indicates how a person changed (or failed to) over the years. History emerges and the lists start to tell stories. The other, non-music-related lists allow for measurement of a certain kind: Did I read more or fewer books, see more or fewer movies than the year before? But I never ranked books and movies the way I did CDs. I might have read certain books in order to review them or because I was doing research for a writing project, but buying music always only had a single purpose: a hope for pleasure. Individual top-ten lists chronicle its attainment, while multiple lists show how my ways of achieving it varied over time. Jazz artists dominate my list from the mid-2000s. In 2004, seven of the ten CDs I picked would be so classified.

Later lists show greater diversity. In 2008, the year I turned forty, I selected only two jazz records (or maybe three, depending on where a collaboration between Willie Nelson and Wynton Marsalis fits). This doesn't indicate any move away from jazz. Rather, it suggests that even in middle age a person continues to go through phases. My 2002 list also had only a couple of jazz albums on it.

6. *Reminders to be humble.* Aware of their own shifting sensibilities, list-makers become less likely to make categorical pronouncements about art. That 2002 list also names two CDs that ended up being sold to a used record dealer and another that fell out of rotation but that I didn't want to sell since friends made it. I can't recall now why I thought OutKast's *Speakerboxxx/The Love Below* was a potential personal classic, or if I ever listened to it after 2003; I do remember deciding it no longer needed to take up space on my shelf. From the start I knew better than to call mine "best of" lists. After a few years I had to acknowledge that what I valued at one moment might not endure. I won't go as far as saying list-making makes one a better, more tolerant person, but it's hard to be dismissive of others' musical taste when confronted with self-generated evidence of fickleness and critical lapses.

7. *Conscious admiration.* While lists may chart changes, they also document what remains stable. Each year's list may bear traces of faddishness or fleeting enthusiasms. But certain names that recur over long stretches of time indicate an artist who really matters. I wasn't aware just how much I liked Elvis Costello until I saw that every album he put out in the 2000s made my top-ten list. Lucinda Williams shows up again and again, too. (Not irrelevantly, Costello and Williams made guest appearances on each others' albums.) And I wouldn't remove Douglas from those old lists if I permitted myself to revise them. Even if artists never learn of my gratitude, I know to whom I would express it if I could.

8. *Serendipity.* New names on top-ten lists spotlight the role luck plays in a person's life. I don't remember how I learned

of Deadboy and the Elephantmen. I didn't put their *We Are Night Sky* on my list in 2005 (presumably because I didn't obtain a copy until 2006), but because of that CD I bought a band member's solo album when it came out in 2007. Dax Riggs's *We Sing Only of Blood or Love* provided one of those thrilling, immediate, single-listen-certainty, this-goes-on-the-list moments. (If Edgar Allan Poe wrote rock and roll lyrics, he might have come up with a mad fever dream like Riggs's "Demon Tied to a Chair in My Brain.") The guitar duo Rodrigo y Gabriela might never have made one of my lists if my wife hadn't happened to see their CD in a store with listening stations, put on headphones and made an unplanned purchase. On *11:11* they pay tribute to artists who inspire them. In my modest, invisible way, that's what I do with my lists, which also commemorate the fortuitousness of my having found these musicians work.

9. *Memento mori.* Lists of artists whose work enriches music lovers' lives eventually become lists of dead people. The music, or some of it, may last, but the makers don't. My 2003 list included posthumous releases by Joe Strummer and Johnny Cash as well as *Tribute to Lester,* the Art Ensemble of Chicago's aural memorial for their dead trumpet player, Lester Bowie. Long-departed geniuses like Monk and Coltrane only ever made my lists because old tapes turned up somewhere. My lists serve as reminders not only to appreciate creative folks when they're alive (as well as afterward), but also to make my own things while I can.

10. *Letters to the future.* Lists preserve something about practices technological developments could radically alter. In the short story "The Sound-Sweep," science fiction writer J.G. Ballard imagines a future when audible music has fallen from favor and people instead prefer ultrasonic music at inaudible frequencies. Even if music that cannot be heard never does reduce musicians like Ballard's Madame Giocanda to tragic obsolescence, immaterial digital files do look likely to make tangible formats like CDs unnecessary artifacts (and

when I no longer bought enough of them to choose from, I stopped making lists). The earlier shift from 78 revolutions-per-minute disks to 33 1/3 rpm long-playing records allowed composers, especially in jazz, to develop longer works than procrustean limits previously allowed. The even greater freedom of the post-platter era could affect how musicians make music. Some might write works longer than could ever have fit on a CD. Then again, perhaps song-by-song releases will turn what I refer to as albums into curiosities. I don't foresee an end to audible music. But albums – sets of deliberately sequenced songs usually of between a half-hour and an hour's duration – might not always be around. For historians and archeologists studying forgotten folkways in times when people receive music differently, top-ten CD lists could be fascinating finds – like recipes for cooking extinct animals. And if that's too grandiose a prediction, then I'll hazard that lists might at least amuse earnest music geeks, who will exist as long as musicians do.

AFTERWORD: A NONBELIEVER'S HOLIDAY WISH LIST

In the spirit of New Year's Eve, a time when people resolve to make improvements in their lives even while knowing that they won't follow through, I'll end with some things I'd like, but don't expect, to see happen.

I'd like for Martin Luther King, Jr., and others who struggled against racial segregation (including atheists like A. Philip Randolph), to be remembered for their actual efforts and achievements. I'd also like for this simple fact to be recognized: religious faith isn't needed to recognize that the lightness or darkness of skin makes no one superior or inferior to anyone else. While his spiritual beliefs might have meant much to Dr. King and many of his supporters, solutions to man-made problems like institutionalized racism are also man-made. Christianity wasn't necessary for people to realize that character and not color counts – and it didn't open the eyes of many faithful racists. King played an instrumental part in pushing the United States closer to the principles of liberty and equality the Founders espoused but the country never realized. The civil rights movement demonstrates human beings' ability to improve their conditions themselves. That's something worth celebrating (and I heartily endorse listening to Mavis Staples sing while doing so).

I'd like for those who recognize the value of love – especially amid the reality of hatred – to orchestrate their own individual expressions of intimacy on whatever days they choose (anniversaries and birthdays being the most obvious choices). Much as the moves to suppress Valentine's Day in places like Iran appall me, the ritualized and, yes, commercialized semi-obligatory exchange of cards and candies troubles me too. Certainly true lovers don't really need an officially designated day to remember to cherish and openly declare their good fortune. (People with honorable parents should acknowledge them on more than just specified days, too, but, really, it's probably not asking too much to call Mom on Mother's Day, which has only artificial, inessential, fully ignorable religious aspects.) And certainly it would be for the best if schools stayed out of this whole Valentine's Day business. (Workplaces, too. Once, when I went regularly to an office, I arrived one morning to discover that every employee had a flower and card waiting on his or her desk. From the boss. It was weird – and rather creepy.)

I'd like to suggest that prizing a literally unbelievable anthology of irreconcilable texts and parading the fantastical wishful thinking derived from it on days like Easter are not the best ways to cope with fears of death. I'd also like to propose that some better books convincingly illustrate that moral behavior does not require belief in any god, and that the study of great works of literature offers a sensible, and rather enjoyable, alternative to endorsement of dogma. (One such work, James Joyce's *Ulysses,* inspired its own sort-of holiday. On Bloomsday – June 16, the day on which the novel is set and the date in 1904 when Joyce first went on a date with the woman he later married – fans of the novel gather and to read aloud their favorite passages or just listen to others read. It's a do-it-yourself kind of celebration open to any lovers of literature who might want to join.) Like Herman Melville does in his April Fools' Day book, I'd like to do openly what some of my old teachers did unwittingly: to encourage doubt and critical thinking rather than credulity and blind faith.

I'd like for those who parade their tribal thinking on days dedicated to ethnic, national and religious identity to realize how this constricts reason and stymies the full flourishing of complex human beings' potential. I can't reduce myself to where I or my ancestors were born, my sexual preferences, the language I speak or the shade of my skin's pigmentation

– or even the combination of these – and I wouldn't try to do so. I'd prefer to topple partitions between people rather than strengthen them.

I'd like to understand what about baseball mesmerizes so many people, but I suspect I never will solve all of life's mysteries. While I've suggested people would be better off without religion, I wouldn't dare recommend they abandon baseball. What would men discuss with their fathers-in-law and barbers? (Then again, boxing once ranked as a favorite subject...) Besides, sports – including baseball – probably have done more than organized religion ever did to foster interracial and international respect, despite what George Orwell might have thought about them. Arguments about presumed racial inferiority have withered when competitors displayed their mettle in games. It's hard to call winners worthless.

I'd like to see Jack Johnson remembered alongside barrier-breaking athletes like Joe Louis, Jesse Owens, Jackie Robinson, Jason Collins and Billie Jean King. Johnson achieved more than a notable historic first by winning the title of heavyweight champion of the world in 1908. When he successfully defended it against the "Great White Hope" Jim Jeffries on Independence Day in 1910, he vividly illustrated vital facts about racism in the United States – and he contributed mightily to the historic change in racial attitudes that took place in the twentieth century. (Johnson also deserves a presidential pardon for the ridiculous 1913 Mann Act conviction. While such a bureaucratic maneuver wouldn't erase the injustice Johnson suffered, it would at least acknowledge both the act's shamefulness and the boxer's blamelessness.) While he was certainly no sporting Martin Luther King or fistic Thomas Jefferson, Johnson in his own way added a compelling chapter to the story of American freedom.

I'd like for the unnecessary religious bits tacked onto secular holidays like Labor Day and May Day to fall away and – as long as I'm indulging ungrounded hopes – for some of the rebelliousness that originally gave rise to such holidays to revive. It seems reasonable to me to let the few truly secular holidays remain nonreligious, and for people to work to improve their conditions in the here and now rather than pin their hopes on something better in an imaginary hereafter.

I'd like for the atrocities committed on September 11, 2001, to be seen as conclusive evidence of the dangers inherent in religious thinking. There's no good reason to deny that religion had anything to do with those events – it plainly did – and there could be no clearer exposure of faith as a faulty moral compass. Mayor Michael Bloomberg made the right call when he excluded religious spokespeople from New York City's official tenth anniversary commemoration and said that the churches were free to organize their own, separate events.

I'd like to promote the exercise of children's – and adults' – creativity and imagination. One small way this could be done would be for Halloween revelers to craft their own costumes and decorations rather than buying them ready-made. I know first-hand what this can do. I've seen it. Along these lines, I also encourage others to devise their own personal, freely chosen traditions and to participate in other quasi-holidays that celebrate creativity, such as Bloomsday (or other days linked with artists or thinkers they admire, such as International Darwin Day in February or International Jazz Day in April). If a holiday doesn't exist that fits with your values as a humanist, freethinker or atheist, make it up (preferably without piggybacking on a religious holiday).

I'd like the act of giving thanks generally (as opposed to thanking particular people) to be recognized as a gesture with religious undertones and implications. Performers of acts and followers of traditions should know what they're doing and why (like Evacuation Day revelers did).

I'd like for celebrants of Christmas and other holy pageants crowding the calendar to stop assuming everyone does, should or will observe their scripturally based or religiously oriented holidays. Just as I don't expect (or even want) anyone to adopt my Beaujolais nouveau tradition, I'd like not to be expected to bow down before beliefs I reject.

Finally, I'd like to raise a glass to my fellow advocates of freedom of thought, freedom of inquiry, freedom of speech and freedom from compulsion to participate in religious rituals.

Cheers.

ACKNOWLEDGMENTS

Though I have reservations about Thanksgiving Day, I eagerly thank those who gave opportunities to ventilate some of my thoughts about holidays and related problems (usually in considerably different form than they appear here). Susan Hansell responded to a simultaneously overlong and undercooked essay on holidays by encouraging me to develop and refine parts of it. Several of the results – "King and Me," "Partitions on Parade" and "Detroit Undead" – subsequently ended up in the journal she edits, *Spot Literary Magazine*. I owe her a large debt of gratitude for her suggestions and patience. Geralda Miller, Demetrice Dalton and Ken Dalton of Our Story Inc. arranged for me to present "Jack Johnson's Fourth of July" as part of events commemorating the 100th anniversary of the Johnson-Jeffries fight in Reno, Nevada, and I thoroughly enjoyed the time I spent with them there. The paper subsequently appeared in *The Nevada Review*, a journal edited by Caleb S. Cage and Joe McCoy. A radically condensed version of "Hollow Eggs and Seeds of Doubt" ran in Atheist Alliance International's *Secular World* magazine, edited by Tom Melchiorre. Peter Werbe of the *Fifth Estate* made recommendations for the shorter iteration, which I appreciate even if those tips aren't reflected here. Showing true class, Caleb Thompson selected "Opening Day Shutout" for *The Monarch Review* despite considering himself a baseball fanatic. Nate Jordon, founder of Monkey Puzzle Press, issued a shorter version of "Christmas Things" as a chapbook suitable for giving as a gift. I also offer my sincere thanks to: Kate Nesheim, in her role as nonfiction editor of *Cream City Review*, where "Ironies on Parade" ran as part of a special "Labor" issue, and Michael J. Thompson and Kurt Jacobsen at *Logos: A Journal of Modern*

Society & Culture (where an earlier, rather different version of the essay appeared under a different title); Adam Garfinkle and Charles Davidson, the editor and publisher, respectively, of *The American Interest* (where a version of "The Overground Railroad Blues" was published beneath another name); Susannah Indigo at *Slow Trains Literary Journal* (which ran an alternate take of "Unbelievable God Songs"); Karen Frantz at the American Humanist Association's *Humanist Network News* ("No Thanks"); Ben LeDoux at *Technicolor Magazine* ("Sir Salman's Day"); Peter Lucas at *Prime Mincer* ("One Hundred and Ten Boxes"); and M. Gonzales at *Meat for Tea: The Valley Review* ("Year-End Top Ten").

For helping to further develop these stories and reflections and for publishing them in this form, I am much obliged to Luis Granados at Humanist Press.

BIBLIOGRAPHY

Amis, Kingsley. *One Fat Englishman* (1963). New York: Signet Books, 1965.

Ashe, Arthur R., Jr. *A Hard Road to Glory: Boxing: The African-American Athlete in Boxing.* New York: Amistad Press, 1988.

Associated Press. "Burmese Poet Arrested for Veiled Protest." *The Guardian.* January 24, 2008. www.guardian.co.uk

Bakhtin, Mikhail. *Rabelais and His Word* (1965), translated by Hélène Iswosky. Bloomington: Indiana University Press, 1984.

Ballard, J.G. *The Complete Short Stories of J.G. Ballard.* New York: W.W. Norton & Co., 2009.

Barnum, Phineas T. *The Life of P.T. Barnum, Written by Himself* (1855). Urbana: University of Chicago Press, 2000.

Batty, David and Peter Walker. "Rushdie knighthood 'justifies suicide attacks.'" *The Guardian.* June 18, 2007. www.guardian.co.uk

Blanshard, Paul. *Freedom and Catholic Power in Spain and Portugal: An American Interpretation.* Boston: Beacon Press, 1962.

Botham, Fay. *Almighty God Created the Races.* Chapel Hill: University of North Carolina Press, 2009.

Bowker, Gordon. *George Orwell.* London: Abacus. 2003.

Boyle, Kevin. *Arc of Justice: A Saga of Race, Civil Rights, and Murder in the Jazz Age.* New York: Picador, 2004.

Buhle, Paul. *Taking Care of Business: Samuel Gompers, George Meany, Lane Kirkland, and the Tragedy of American Labor.* New York: Monthly Review Press, 1999.

Campbell, Duncan and Vikram Dodd. "Rushdie Knighthood Rekindles 18-year-old Controversy." *The Guardian.* June 19, 2007. www.guardian.co.uk

Camus, Albert. *The Myth of Sisyphus & Other Essays*, translated by Justin O'Brien. New York: Vintage Books, 1955.

Chernow, Ron. *Alexander Hamilton*. New York: The Penguin Press, 2004.

Coleman, R. Leigh. "Anne Graham Lotz on the Wake-Up Call of 9/11: 'Signs of the Times' Revealed." *The Christian Post*. September 10, 2011. www.christianpost

Delbanco, Andrew. *Melville: His World and Work*. New York: Alfred A. Knopf, 2005.

DeLillo, Don. *Mao II*. New York: Viking, 1991.

DeWan, George. "America Celebrates Its New Freedom: Defeated British and Loyalists board ships to leave the U.S." *Newsday*, November 20, 2007. www.newsday.com.

Douthat, Ross. "They Made America," *The Atlantic Monthly*, December 2006.

Ehrenreich, Barbara. *Dancing in the Streets: A History of Collective Joy*. New York: Metropolitan Books, 2007.

Ellis, Joseph J. *American Creation: Triumphs and Tragedies at the Founding of the Republic*. New York: Alfred A. Knopf, 2007.

—. *Founding Brothers: The Revolutionary Generation* (New York: Vintage Books, 2000.

Flynn, Tom. "Matthew vs. Luke: Whoever Wins, Coherence Loses." *Free Inquiry*, Vol. 25, No, 1, 2004.

—. *The Trouble with Christmas*. Amherst, NY: Prometheus Books, 1992.

Foner, Eric. *The Story of American Freedom*. New York: W.W. Norton & Co., 1998.

Gaines, James R. *For Liberty and Glory: Washington, Lafayette, and Their Revolutions* (New York: W.W. Norton & Co., 2007.

Goodwin, Doris Kearns. *Team of Rivals: The Political Genius of Abraham Lincoln*. New York: Simon & Schuster, 2005.

Gould, Stephen Jay. *The Richness of Life: The Essential Stephen Jay Gould*, edited by Steven Rose. New York: W.W. Norton & Co., 2007.

Greenberg, David. "The Pledge of Allegiance: Why We're Not One Nation 'Under God.'" *Slate*, June 28, 2002. www.slate. com

Greenblatt, Stephen. *Will in the World: How Shakespeare Became Shakespeare*. New York: W.W. Norton & Co., 2004.

Harris, Sam. *The End of Faith: Religion, Terror, and the Future of Reason*. New York: W.W. Norton & Co., 2004.

Hauser, Thomas. *The Lost Legacy of Muhammad Ali*. Toronto: Sport Classic Books. 2005.

History.com. "The History of Valentine's Day." Undated. www.history.com

Hitchens, Christopher. "Assassins of the Mind." *Vanity Fair*. February 2009.

— (ed.). *The Portable Atheist: Essential Reading for the Nonbeliever*. Philadelphia: Da Capo Press, 2007.

—. *Letters to a Young Contrarian*. New York: Basic Books, 2001.

Hobsbawm, Eric. "Birth of a Holiday: The First of May" in *Uncommon People: Resistance, Rebellion and Jazz*. New York: The New Press, 1998.

Homer. *The Odyssey*, translated by Richard Lattimore. New York: Harper & Row, 1968.

—. *The Iliad*, translated by Robert Fitzgerald. Garden City, NY: Anchor Books, 1974.

Juneteenth.com. "History of Juneteenth." Undated. www.juneteenth.com

King-Hammond, Leslie. "Jacob Lawrence and the Aesthetic Ethos of the Harlem Working-Class Community" in *Over the Line: The Art and Life of Jacob Lawrence*, edited by Peter T. Nesbett and Michelle DuBois. Seattle: University of Washington Press, 2000.

Klausen, Jytte. *The Cartoons that Shook the World*. New Haven: Yale University Press, 2009.

Kolodner, Meredith. "CLC Rains on Own Labor Day Parade," *The Chief*, August 17, 2007.

Lahiri, Jhumpa. *Unaccustomed Earth*. New York: Alfred A. Knopf, 2008.

Lamott, Anne. "Why I Hate Mother's Day." *Salon*. May 8, 2013. www.salon.com

Larkin, Philip. *Collected Poems*. New York: Farrar, Strauss and Giroux, 2004.

Liebling, A.J. *A Neutral Corner*, edited by Fred Warner and James Barbour. San Francisco: North Point Press, 1990.

—. *The Sweet Science* (1956). New York: North Point Press, 2004.

LifeWay. "Mother's Day Church Attendance Third among Holidays, Father's Day Last." May 11, 2012. www.lifeway.com

Lincoln, Abraham. "Thanksgiving Day Proclamation, October 3, 1863." www.nps.gov

Lipset, Seymour Martin and Gary Marks, *It Didn't Happen Here: Why Socialism Failed in the United States*. New York: W.W. Norton & Co., 2000.

Lukas, J. Anthony. *Big Trouble: A Murder in a Small Western Town Sets off a Struggle for the Soul of America*. New York: Simon & Schuster, 1997.

Mailer, Norman. *Miami and the Siege of Chicago: An Informal History of the Republican and Democratic Conventions of 1968*. New York: New York Review Books, 2008.

—. *Cannibals and Christians*. New York: The Dial Press, 1966.

Maliszewski, Paul. *Fakers: Hoaxers, Con Artists, Counterfeiters, and Other Great Pretenders*. New York: The New Press. 2008.

Maugham, W. Somerset. *Of Human Bondage* (1915). New York: Penguin Books, 1981.

McCrum, Robert. "Don DeLillo: 'I'm not trying to manipulate reality – this is what I see and hear.'" *The Observer*. August 7, 2010. www.observer.guardian.co.uk

McMillen, Neil R. *The Citizens' Council*. Champaign: University of Illinois Press, 1994.

Mead, Chris. *Champion: Joe Louis - Black Hero in White America*. London: Robson Books, 1986.

Melville, Herman. *The Confidence-Man: His Masquerade*. (1857), edited by Hershel Parker. New York: W.W. Norton & Co. 1971.

—. *Moby-Dick* (1851), edited by Harrison Hayford and Hershel Parker. New York: W.W. Norton & Co. 1967.

Newfield, Jack. *Somebody's Gotta Tell It: The Upbeat Memoir of a Working-Class Journalist*. New York: St. Martin's Press, 2002.

Orwell, George. "Reflections on Gandhi" (1949). *Essays*. New York: Everyman Books, 2002.

—. "The Sporting Spirit" (1945). *Essays*. New York: Everyman Books, 2002.

Paine, Thomas. *The American Crisis: 16 Revolutionary War Pamphlets*. Rockville, MD: Wildside Press, 2010.

Pfeffer, Paula A. *A. Philip Randolph, Pioneer of the Civil Rights Movement* (1990). Baton Rouge: Louisiana State University Press, 1996.

Pew Forum on Religion & Public Life. "'Nones' on the Rise: One in Five Adults Have No Religious Affiliation." October 9, 2012. www.pewforum.org

—. "U.S. Religious Knowledge Survey: Who Knows What about Religion." September 28, 2010. www.pewforum.org

Ratliff, Ben. *Coltrane: The Story of a Sound*. New York: Farrar, Strauss and Giroux, 2007.

Roberts, Randy. *Papa Jack: Jack Johnson and the Era of White Hopes*. New York: The Free Press, 1983.

Rushdie, Salman. *Joseph Anton: A Memoir*. New York: Random House. 2012.

—. *The Enchantress of Florence*. New York: Random House, 2008.

—. *Shalimar the Clown*. New York: Random House, 2005.

—. "February 1999: Ten Years of the Fatwa." *Step across This Line: Collected Nonfiction 1992 - 2002*. New York: Random House, 2002.

—. *The Ground Beneath Her Feet*. New York: Henry Holt and Company, 1999.

—. *Imaginary Homelands: Essays and Criticism 1981 – 1991* (1991). New York: Penguin Books, 1992.

—. *The Satanic Verses*. New York: Viking, 1988.

Salvatore, Nick. *Eugene V. Debs: Citizen and Socialist*. Urbana: University of Illinois Press, 1984.

Sandomir, Richard. "Baseball Continued: Between Rebirth and Calamity." *The New York Times*. September 24, 2010. www.nytimes.com

Santella, Andrew. "Thanks, but No Thanks." *Slate*. November 19, 2007. www.slate.com

Schulberg, Budd. *Sparring with Hemingway: And Other Legends of the Fight Game*. Chicago: Ivan R. Dee, 1995.

Schwartz, Stephen and Irfan al-Alawi. "Valentine's Day in Saudi Arabia: Portents of Change from the Desert Kingdom." *The Weekly Standard*, Vol. 12, No. 24, March 5, 2007. www.weeklystandard.com

Sen, Amartya. *Identity and Violence: The Illusion of Destiny*. New York: W.W. Norton & Co., 2006.

Shange, Ntozake. *Sassafrass, Cypress & Indigo*. New York: St. Martin's Press, 1982.

Sohn, Emily. "Did President Lincoln Believe in God?" *Discovery News*. April 15, 2011. www.news.discovery.com

Speckhardt, Roy. "Keeping Our Human Light Lit During the Holidays: HumanLight Is about Celebrating and Expressing What Fills our Lives with Love and Meaning." *Patheos*. December 9, 2012. www.patheos.com

Stone, Geoffrey R. *Perilous Times: Free Speech in Wartime: From the Sedition Act of 1798 to the War on Terrorism*. New York: W.W. Norton & Co., 2004.

Stone, Michael. "Secular Americans Praise Bloomberg – 9/11 Ceremony Religion Free." *Examiner.com*. September 11, 2011. www.examiner.com

—. "NY Mayor Bloomberg Bans Religion at 9/11 Ceremony." *Examiner.com*. August 25, 2011. www.examiner.com

Talese, Gay. *The Silent Season of a Hero: The Sports Writing of Gay Talese*, edited by Michael Rosenwald. New York: Walker & Co., 2010.

Theoharis, Jeanne. *The Rebellious Life of Mrs. Rosa Parks*. Boston: Beacon Press, 2013.

Twain, Mark. *Pudd'nhead Wilson* (1894), edited by Sidney Berger. New York: W.W. Norton & Co., 2005.

U.S. Census Bureau. "Facts for Features: Valentine's Day: February 14." February 7, 2006. www.census.gov

Virgil. *The Aeneid*, translated by Allen Mandelbaum. New York: Bantam Books, 1985.

Vonnegut, Kurt. *Breakfast of Champions*. New York: Delacorte Press, 1973.

Ward, Geoffrey C. *Unforgivable Blackness: The Rise and Fall of Jack Johnson*. New York: Alfred A. Knopf, 2004.

Weinberg, Arthur and Lila Weinberg. *Clarence Darrow: A Sentimental Rebel*. New York: Atheneum, 1987.

Wilkerson, Isabel. *The Warmth of Other Suns: The Epic Story of America's Great Migration*. New York: Random House, 2010.